GERMAN FIGHTER AIRCRAFT
OF WORLD WAR II
1939–45

GERMAN FIGHTER AIRCRAFT
OF WORLD WAR II
1939–45

THOMAS NEWDICK

amber
BOOKS

Reprinted in 2022, 2024

This Amber edition first published in 2020

Published by Amber Books Ltd
United House
London N7 9DP
United Kingdom
www.amberbooks.co.uk
Facebook: amberbooks
YouTube: amberbooksltd
Instagram: amberbooksltd
X(Twitter): @amberbooks

ISBN: 978-1-78274-970-7

Editor: Michael Spilling
Designer: Andrew Easton
Picture research: Terry Forshaw

Printed in China

Contents

Introduction

The German Luftwaffe had been reborn in the interwar period as an air arm primarily designed to offer support to German ground forces – the Wehrmacht. When war broke out in Europe in September 1939, it was the Germany Army that spearheaded the *Blitzkrieg* ('lightning war') campaign throughout the continent, while the Luftwaffe provided air cover and ground support.

At the start of the conflict, the Luftwaffe had, in the Messerschmitt Bf 109, what was probably the finest single-engine fighter in service anywhere in the world at that time. While its armament was slightly inferior to that of the Royal Air Force's Supermarine Spitfire, the Bf 109 had been operationally proven during the Spanish Civil War, where the Luftwaffe had had the opportunity to develop and refine tactics more advanced than those of the RAF as of 1939. In common with the Spitfire, the Bf 109 underwent constant refinement throughout the war and remained the most important type equipping the *Jagdverband* (Fighter Arm) until the very end of fighting In Europe.

The other standout single-seat fighter design fielded by Germany was the Focke-Wulf Fw 190, which appeared in service in 1941 and was broadly equivalent to the RAF's Hawker Typhoon. The Fw 190 excelled in the air-to-air role, but as the tides of the war turned it found itself increasingly employed as a *Sturmjäger* (assault fighter), blurring the distinction between fighter and bomber as it

Messerschmitt Me 210A-2 heavy fighters from the *Stabsschwarm* (staff) of III./ZG 1 fly low over the Tunisian countryside in 1943. Only a small number of units used Me 210s before the improved Me 410 entered service.

took over from the Junkers Ju 87 dive-bomber that had proved to be hopelessly vulnerable when confronted by modern fighter opposition.

Versatile force

The airmen and equipment of the *Jagdverband* were required to demonstrate great versatility throughout the war, as the conflict moved between widely differing theatres and the nature of the fighting evolved. Up until the Battle of Britain, the Luftwaffe's fighters had been required, almost exclusively, to patrol the skies over the battlefield, where the front lines were often moving rapidly.

By the time the tables had turned in the air war over the United Kingdom in late 1940, Luftwaffe fighters were flying bomber escort; and from 1942 onwards, as the Allied bomber offensive gathered pace, German aircraft were increasingly called upon to defend the Reich against massed enemy formations. A lack of range and armament afflicted the single-seat

fighters in particular, but more often than not the heaviest losses were due to employing aircraft in roles for which they had not been designed. The addition of yet more weapons – and therefore more weight – also had a negative effect on the performance of Germany's fighters.

'Ace of aces'

Despite these challenges, German fighter pilots racked up extraordinary combat records, with no fewer than 15 men gaining more than 200 combat victories. While most of these were scored on the Eastern Front, the leading Luftwaffe ace in North Africa, Hans-Joachim Marseille, destroyed 158 RAF and Commonwealth aircraft, all while flying the Bf 109. By contrast, the highest-scoring Allied pilot, Soviet flyer Ivan Kozhedub, acheived 62 solo victories. Meanwhile, Germany's 'ace of aces' was Erich Hartmann, who assembled a tally of 352 victories in the space of three-and-a-half years – a total likely to never be surpassed.

Only two jet-powered Messerschmitt Me 262A-1a/ U4s were completed, each featuring a huge 50mm (1.97in) Mauser MK 214A cannon in the nose. Like many weapons in Germany's special weapons' programme, the production version never came to fruition.

7

BIPLANES

In terms of aircraft performance, complexity and lethality, the 1930s was a time of massive improvement in fighters, reflected in the rapid advances made by the German aeronautical industry. While the appearance of the superlative Messerschmitt Bf 109 quickly replaced the biplane equipment, biplane fighters survived in Luftwaffe service long enough to see use during World War II, though in most cases they had been relegated by now to secondary duties – including training – or to less critical theatres where enemy fighter opposition was less potent.

This chapter includes the following aircraft:

- Heinkel He 51
- Arado Ar 66
- Arado Ar 68
- Fiat CR.42 *Falco*

The Heinkel He 51B-2 twin-float biplane enjoyed a relatively long career as a fighter trainer. A total of 46 such aircraft were delivered to the 1. And 2. Staffeln of Küstenjagdgruppe 136, where they replaced the obsolete Heinkel He 38.

Heinkel He 51

The lineage of the He 51 – regarded as the Luftwaffe's first true fighter – stretches back to the He 49a, a single-seat biplane first flown in November 1932. In contrast to the He 51 that followed, the He 49a was, ostensibly at least, a civilian advanced trainer.

Heinkel He 51B-1

This aircraft served in the fighter training role with A/B Schule 123 at Agram (Zagreb) in the spring of 1942.

There were another two prototypes: the He 49b with an extended fuselage and the He 49c with faired landing gear. Experience with the He 49 led directly to the He 51a, first flown in summer 1933. Next came a pre-production batch of nine He 51A-0 aircraft completed to the same standard and delivered from spring 1934, before the aircraft entered full-scale production as the He 51A-1. The first of these were delivered to the Luftwaffe in April 1935 and a total of 150 examples were built, by both Heinkel and Arado.

It was examples of the He 51A-1 that equipped the Luftwaffe's first fighter unit, Jagdgeschwader 'Richthofen', when the first examples were taken on strength by II./JG 132 in April 1935, before replacing the Ar 65E with I./JG 132 by the end of the year.

Once the airframe had been subjected to structural refinements, the aircraft was re-designated as the He 51B. This model was completed both as a landplane (He 51B-0, 12

built) and as a floatplane fighter that could be launched by catapult from warships (He 51B-2, 38 built).

The land-based He 51B-0 succeeded the He 51A on the production line in January 1936 while the He 51B-2 also had provision to carry out offensive missions, armed with racks for up to six 10kg (22lb) bombs; it served with the 1. and 2. Staffeln of Küstenjagdgruppe 136. The last of the B-series was the He 51B-3 that had longer-span wings for optimized high-altitude performance; only a single example was completed.

Spanish service

By 1936 the Heinkel design was the most important fighter in Luftwaffe service, and it saw combat with the Condor Legion during the Spanish Civil War from August that year and was also used by the Nationalist forces in the same conflict. In Spain, the He 51 was operated by the

Condor Legion's Jagdgruppe 88 (3. Staffeln) and by the Nationalist 1-E-2 and 2-E-2 squadrons. After initially operating in a fighter capacity, the arrival of more advanced opposition on the Republican side, such as the Polikarpov I-16, forced the He 51 increasingly into a dive-bombing and close support role.

Heinkel He 51B-1

Weight (Maximum take-off) 1900kg (4189lb)

Dimensions Length: 8.4m (27ft 7in), Wingspan: 11m (36ft 1in), Height: 3.2m (10ft 6in)

Powerplant One 559kW (750hp) BMW VI 7.3 Z V-12 liquid-cooled piston engine

Speed 330km/h (210mph)

Range 570 km (350 miles)

Ceiling 7700m (25,300ft)

Crew 2

Armament Two 7.92mm (0.31in) MG 17 machine guns in nose; six 10kg (22lb) bombs (C-1)

Heinkel He 51B-1
This aircraft also served as a fighter trainer with A/B Schule 71 at Prossnitz (Prostejov) in 1942.

Developed specifically for service in Spain was the ground-attack-optimized He 51C series, all of which had modifications to allow carriage of up to four 50kg (110lb) bombs. The initial He 51C-1 was complemented by the He 51C-2, which had improved radio equipment. A total of 100 C-models were completed by Fieseler.

Production breakdown was 79 He 51C-1s (51 for the Nationalists and 28 for the Condor Legion) and 21 He 51C-2s that served with German coastal defence units. After its frontline duties had come to an end, the He 51 remained in use as a training aircraft, the final examples still serving in this role in 1942–43.

Three of the nine He 51A-0 pre-production machines – He 51A-01 D-IQEE, A-04 D-IJAY and A-05 D-IDIE – that were delivered from April 1934. The He 51A-0s were initially used for covert trials by the military, so wore civil markings and registrations, with no swastikas.

Arado Ar 66

Walter Rethel's final design for Arado before he made the switch to Messerschmitt, the Ar 66 was a single-bay biplane of mixed construction that began to be delivered to the Luftwaffe in 1933.

Following Rethel's departure from the firm, responsibility for continued development fell upon Walter Blume. The Ar 66 was characterized by its swept-back wing panels, long-chord ailerons on both the upper and lower wings and an unorthodox tail unit that featured a strut-braced tailplane mounted on an elevated rear fuselage fairing in front of the vertical tail surface. The entirety of the vertical tail was a rudder, with no fixed fin area.

Trainer aircraft

The type was introduced as the Ar 66C, a two-seat primary and basic trainer, which remained in service at the outbreak of World War II. The Ar 66a prototype flown in 1932 was followed by a seaplane version, the Ar 66b, with a pair of side-by-side wooden floats and a rudder enlarged via the introduction of an extension below the bottom of the sternpost

Arado Ar 66C

Arado Ar 66C, NJ+AC was based at Pori, Finland, in January 1944. The aircraft served with Nachtschlachtgruppe 8 (NSGr 8), a night-harassment unit. The same group also flew examples of the Junkers Ju 87.

and a ventral fin ahead of it. Ten production Ar 66B floatplanes were built but the bulk of the production run comprised Ar 66C versions, powered by a single Argus As 10C inverted-Vee engine rated at 179kW (240hp) and used to equip military and civilian flying schools. These aircraft saw frontline duties from 1943, when they were pressed into service as night ground-attack aircraft. Operating on the Eastern Front, they flew alongside Gotha Go 145 trainers within *Störkampfstaffeln* night harassment units, typically armed with 2kg and 4kg (4.4lb and 8.8lb) anti-personnel bomblets.

Arado Ar 66C

Weight (Maximum take-off) 1330kg (2932lb)
Dimensions Length: 8.3m (27ft 3in), Wingspan: 10m (32ft 10in), Height: 2.93m (9ft 7in)
Powerplant One 179kW (240hp) Argus As 10C inverted-V engine
Speed 210km/h (130mph)
Range 716km (445 miles)
Ceiling 4500m (14,800ft)
Crew 2
Armament 2kg (4.4lb) and 4kg (8.8lb) bomblets

Arado Ar 68

The Ar 68, which was the final biplane fighter type to enter Luftwaffe service, traced its origins back to the Ar 67, a single example of which was first flown in late 1933. This was a mixed-construction biplane fighter powered by a 477kW (640hp) Rolls-Royce Kestrel VI engine.

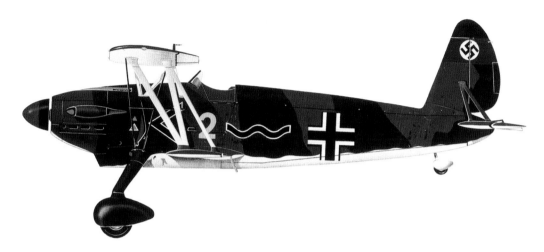

The subsequent Ar 68a prototype first flew in summer 1934, powered by a BMW VId 12-cylinder Vee engine developing 410kW (550hp). Performance was disappointing. An improvement came with the Ar 68b powered by a supercharged 455kW (610hp) Junkers Jumo 210 12-cylinder inverted-Vee engine, providing additional power and an improved forward field of vision for the pilot. Nevertheless, the chin radiator had a detrimental effect on performance.

Fighter armament

The b-model was followed by the Ar 68c that featured a redesigned radiator and, for the first time, armament of two fixed, forward-firing 7.92mm (0.31in) MG 17 machine guns. The Ar 68c was first flown in summer 1935. Last of the prototypes were the Ar 68d and Ar 68e, powered respectively by the

Arado Ar 68E

Piloted by Lieutenant Riegel, the unit's *Gruppenadjutant*, this Arado Ar 68E served with III./Jagdgeschwader 141, based at Fürstenwalde in 1938.

BMW VI and Jumo 210 and which served as pre-production aircraft.

Arado's new biplane went into service with the Luftwaffe in late summer 1936, the initial examples of the Ar 68F-1 going to I./JG 134 'Horst Wessel'. These aircraft were powered by the 570kW (750hp) BMW VI engine, although it had been intended for the Jumo-engined E-model to become the standard production version.

Ar 68E-1

A refined production version became available in spring 1937, when the Ar 68E-1 began to be delivered, its appearance delayed by a shortage of

Arado Ar 68E

Weight (Maximum take-off) 2020kg (4453lb)
Dimensions Length: 9.5m (31ft 2in), Wingspan: 11m (36ft 1in), Height: 3.3m (10ft 10in)
Powerplant One 455kW (610hp) Jumo 210Da engine
Speed 330km/h (210mph)
Range 500km (310 miles)
Ceiling 7400m (24,300ft)
Crew 2
Armament Two 7.92mm (0.31in) MG 17 machine guns; six 10kg (22lb) bombs

the required Jumo 210 engines. This version could also carry offensive armament – a rack for six 10kg (22lb) bombs under the fuselage. Minor differences were incorporated in the Ar 68E-1 in the form of power provided either by the Jumo 210Da or the subsequent Jumo 210Ea engine, although power output was similar.

A further improved Ar 68H with 634kW (850hp) BMW 132 nine-cylinder radial engine, enclosed cockpit and enhanced firepower in the shape of two more MG 17 machine guns in the leading edge of the upper wing didn't progress beyond the prototype stage. This version would have provided a boost in speed by 65km/h (41mph).

The Ar 68G, which was never built, would have been powered by a supercharged BMW engine.

Efficient design

Overall, the Ar 68 offered a good level of aerodynamic efficiency for its time. Construction was based around an oval-section fuselage fabricated from steel tubes and covered by light alloy panels on the forward section and rear decking; the remainder of the fuselage was covered with fabric. Wooden-construction wings were of the single-bay type and were covered with a combination of plywood and fabric. The tail unit included a distinctively shaped vertical surface, the design of which would become standard on subsequent Arado designs in this class.

Trainer

Two examples of the Ar 68E-1 were involved in operational trials during the Spanish Civil War in 1938. However, by the outbreak of World War II most surviving Ar 68s had been relegated to advanced fighter training duties with the Luftwaffe's various *Jagdfliegerschulen* (fighter pilot schools).

A small number served as interim night-fighters pending the arrival of dedicated equipment.

Arado Ar 68F

Assigned to 3./Jagdgeschwader 135, this Ar 68F was based at Bad Aibling during 1937.

Arado Ar 68F

Weight (Maximum take-off) 2020kg (4453lb)
Dimensions Length: 9.5m (31ft 2in), Wingspan: 11m (36ft 1in), Height: 3.3m (10ft 10in)
Powerplant One 541kW (725hp) BMW VI V-12 liquid-cooled piston engine
Speed 330km/h (210mph)
Range 500km (310 miles)
Ceiling 7400m (24,300ft)
Crew 2
Armament Two 7.92mm (0.31in) MG 17 machine guns; Six 10kg (22lb) bombs

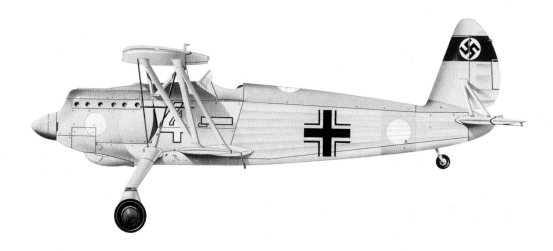

Fiat CR.42 *Falco*

Designed by Celestino Rosatelli, the CR.42 *Falco* ('Falcon') was first flown on 23 May 1938. By the time production came to an end in late 1942, a total of 1781 of these unequal-span biplane fighters had been completed, including examples exported to Belgium, Hungary and Sweden.

Fiat CR.42 Falco

This CR.42 flew with 2. Staffel, Nachtschlachtgruppe 9, in the Rimini area of northern Italy in early 1944.

By the time of the Italian surrender on 7 September 1943, 113 aircraft remained on strength, although only 64 of these were serviceable.

German service

Some of these were taken on charge by the Luftwaffe and were engaged on operations in the north of the country, primarily taking part in anti-partisan operations. The aircraft undertook night harassment missions in the area around Rimini in early 1944, known units including the 2. Staffel of Nachtschlachtgruppe 9. Other examples are reported to have operated in Austria and Yugoslavia, where they were employed in similar missions. Fiat's production figures for the CR.42 also show that 150 aircraft were completed for the Luftwaffe for

night ground-attack duties during 1943–44, under the designation CR.42LW (for Luftwaffe).

Derived from the Fiat CR.32, the *Falco* retained its wing configuration but introduced a radial engine. The aircraft's basic structure was metal, with a covering of fabric and light alloy. The wide-track tailwheel undercarriage featured oleo-pneumatic shock absorbers and leg and wheel fairings for the main gear, although these were sometimes discarded in Luftwaffe service. Power was provided by a Fiat A.74 R1C.38 radial engine in a long-chord cowling. The CR.42LW could carry a bombload of two 100kg (220lb) weapons mounted on underwing racks. Gun armament comprised two or four 12.7mm (0.5in) Breda-SAFAT machine guns.

Fiat CR.42 Falco
Weight (Maximum take-off) 2295kg (5060lb)
Dimensions Length: 8.25m (27ft 1in), Wingspan: 9.7m (31ft 10in), Height: 3.585m (11ft 9in)
Powerplant One 627kW (841hp) Fiat A.74 R1C.38 14 cylinder air-cooled radial piston engine
Speed 441km/h (274mph)
Range 780km (480 miles)
Ceiling 10,210m (33,500ft)
Crew 1
Armament Two 12.7mm (0.5in) Breda-SAFAT machine guns; two 100kg (220lb) bombs on underwing racks

SINGLE-SEAT MONOPLANES

The superb Messerschmitt Bf 109 enabled the Germans to gain substantial aerial supremacy early in the war and it was later joined by the Focke-Wulf Fw 190, which again greatly assisted the advance of the Wehrmacht. Although the Luftwaffe experimented with other single-engine piston fighters, none would enter full-scale production for domestic use, a reflection of the basic quality of the Bf 109 and Fw 190 family. This chapter includes:

- Heinkel He 112
- Heinkel He 100
- Messerschmitt Bf 109
- Focke-Wulf Fw 190
- Focke-Wulf Ta 152
- Dewoitine D.520
- Dornier Do 335 *Pfeil*
- Blohm und Voss BV 40

Messerschmitt Bf 109s being serviced. Like its great rival, the Royal Air Force's Spitfire, the Messerschmitt fighter underwent continuous improvement throughout World War II and remained the cornerstone of the *Jagdverband* right up to the end.

Heinkel He 112

The He 112 emerged from a Luftwaffe requirement to replace the biplane He 51 and Ar 68 fighters and a specification was drawn up by the *Reichsluftfahrtministerium* (German Air Ministry) in 1933.

Submissions were received from Arado, Focke-Wulf, Heinkel and Messerschmitt and all were evaluated at Travemünde in October 1935. Heinkel's offering was the He 112 powered by a 518kW (695hp) Rolls-Royce Kestrel V. Ten examples were ordered for trials and included two with reduced-span wings and 447kW (600hp) Jumo 210C engines. The fourth featured a revised, elliptical wing and was sent to Spain for operational trials in 1936.

In the event, the Luftwaffe rejected the proposed He 112A production aircraft in favour of the Messerschmitt Bf 109, which became the service's standard monoplane fighter. Nevertheless, Heinkel refused to give up on the He 112 and a structural redesign led to the He 112B with a

507kW (680hp) Jumo 210Ea engine, first flown in July 1937. The B-model was armed with a pair of 20mm (0.8in) MG FF cannons in the wings and two 7.92mm (0.31in) MG 17 machine guns in the upper engine cowling.

A batch of 30 He 112Bs were ordered by Japan but only 12 were delivered in spring 1938 before production was redirected to the Luftwaffe. Of these Luftwaffe aircraft, 11 were then handed over to the Spanish Nationalists, who later received the final batch of six aircraft in November 1938.

Thirteen He 112B-0 and 11 He 112B-1 aircraft were delivered to Romania by September 1939 and three more He 112B-1s were acquired by Hungary in spring 1939.

Heinkel He 112B-1

A Romanian Air Force He 112B-1 of the Flotilei 1 Vânatoare (1st Fighter Squadron), based at Bucharest in early 1940.

Heinkel He 112B-1

Weight (Maximum take-off) 2230kg (4916lb)
Dimensions Length: 9m (29ft 6in), Wingspan: 11.5m (37ft 9in), Height: 3.7m (12ft 2in)
Powerplant One 507kW (680hp) Jumo 210Ea engine
Speed 488km/h (303mph)
Range 1100km (680 miles)
Ceiling 8000m (26,000ft)
Crew 2
Armament Two 20mm (0.8in) MG FF cannons and two 7.92mm (0.31in) machine guns

---

Heinkel He 100

While the He 112 never entered large-scale production, designers Heinrich Hertel and Siegfried Günter persevered and drafted a new aircraft optimized for high speed.

The He 100a prototype took to the air on 22 January 1938 powered by a Daimler-Benz DB 601 engine. Intended to reach a speed of 700km/h

(435mph), the He 100a was also tailored for ease of production, with a limited number of curved components and reduced number

of parts in comparison with contemporary designs.

The second prototype was equipped with a DB 601M engine

and captured the 100km (62-mile) closed-circuit landplane record on 6 June 1938, in the hands of Ernst Udet. This aircraft was also referred to as the He 112U, with the aim of promoting export interest in the He 112.

The third He 100 was outfitted with a streamlined cockpit canopy, reduced-span wing and a boosted DB 601 engine, with the aim of taking the absolute world speed record. It crashed in September 1938 and was replaced by the eighth prototype, in which Hans Dieterle recorded a speed of 746.61km/h (463.92mph) at Oranienburg on 30 March 1939. The fourth and fifth He 100s were He

100B variants, while the sixth, seventh and ninth were He 100Cs. Of the C-models, the first was equipped with two 20mm MG FF cannons and four 7.92mm (0.31in) MG 17 machine guns.

Redesign

Handling problems led to a redesign and the appearance of the He 100D with enlarged tail surfaces and a semi-retractable radiator. Armed with an MG FF and two MG 17s, 15 He 100Ds were built: three pre-production He 100D-0s and 12 production He 100D-1s. Their service use was limited to local defence of the Heinkel factory at Rostock.

Heinkel He 100D-1

Weight (Maximum take-off) 2500kg (5512lb)
Dimensions Length: 8.20m (26ft 11in), Wingspan: 9.40m (30ft 10in), Height: 3.60m (11ft 10in)
Powerplant One 876kW (1175hp) Daimler-Benz DB 601M liquid-cooled V12 piston engine
Speed 670km/h (420mph)
Range 1010km (630 miles)
Ceiling 11,000m (36,000ft)
Crew 2
Armament One 20mm (0.8in) MG FF cannon and two 7.92mm (0.31in) MG 17 machine guns

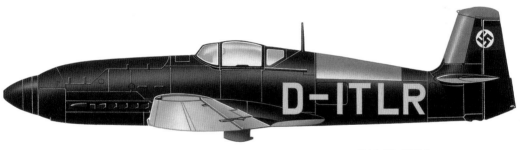

Heinkel He 100D-0

The first of the pre-series He 100D-0 aircraft, D-ITLR, was later sold to Japan. It was alternatively designated as the He 100 V10 (the last of the prototype V series) and began flight testing in September 1939.

Heinkel He 100V-2

The second prototype, He 100 V2, D-IUOS, was flown by the legendary pilot Ernst Udet to capture the 100km (62-mile) closed-circuit landplane record on 6 June 1938.

Messerschmitt Bf 109 prototypes

The superlative Bf 109 emerged from the build-up of the Luftwaffe as a modern air arm in the mid-1930s. After developing expertise in monoplane design with the Bf 108 four-seater, Willy Messerschmitt turned his attention to design of a single-seat fighter.

At the time, Messerschmitt himself was apparently less than confident that his company would win against more established firms and, with little to lose, took the opportunity to incorporate a range of advanced design features. The resulting Bf 109 fought off competition from the Arado Ar 80 and Focke-Wulf Fw 159 before it, together with the Heinkel He 112, was selected for further evaluation, pre-production batches of 10 of each eventually being ordered.

As first flown sometime towards the end of May 1935, the initial Bf 109 V1 was powered by an interim Rolls-Royce Kestrel engine producing 518kW (695hp). The maiden flight was in the hands of test pilot Hans-Dietrich Knötsch at Haunstetten after which official trials began at Rechlin, where the V1 demonstrated better speed and handling than its Heinkel rival.

Prototype batches

The second prototype, Bf 109 V2, replaced the Kestrel with the planned 455kW (610hp) Junkers Jumo 210A and took to the air in early January 1936.

The prototype batch of Bf 109s were used for trials of a variety of different armament combinations. The V2 was the first to be armed, with two 7.92mm (0.31in) MG 17 machine guns in the fuselage upper decking. Meanwhile, Bf 109 V3, flown in June 1936, added provision for an engine-mounted 20mm (0.8in) MG FF cannon.

Sometimes known as Bf 109As, the three Bf 109 prototypes were all assigned civilian registrations, D-IABI, D-IUDE and D-IOQY for aircraft V1, V2 and V3 respectively.

Messerschmitt Bf 109 V10

Flown by Ernst Udet at the International Flying Meeting, the tenth prototype of the Bf 109 was powered by a racing DB 600 engine. Outstandingly fast for its day, the V10 crash-landed during the Circuit of the Alps race, its engine having been pressed too hard.

D-IOQY was the third Bf 109 prototype, and the first to feature provision for an engine armament. Powered by a Jumo 210 engine, the aircraft was one of three sent to Spain in December 1936 for combat trials.

Messerschmitt Bf 109B/C/D

The 10 pre-production Bf 109s were completed as Bf 109B-0s, each of which received a corresponding *Versuchs* (test) number from V4 to V13. At the same time, these aircraft were designated Bf 109B-01, B-02 and so on.

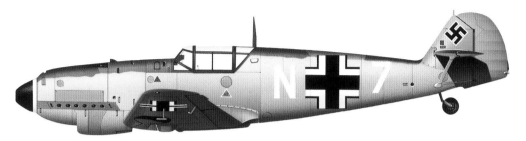

Messerschmitt Bf 109D

Weight (Maximum take-off) 2296kg (5062lb)

Dimensions Length: 8.55m (28ft 1in), Wingspan: 9.87m (32ft 4in), Height: 2.45m (8ft)

Powerplant One 474kW (635hp) Jumo 210Da inverted-V engine

Speed 520km/h (323mph)

Range 650km (405 miles)

Ceiling 10,500m (34,450ft)

Crew 2

Armament Four 7.92mm (0.31in) MG 17 machine guns (two in wings, two in nose)

Messerschmitt Bf 109D

Oberleutnant Johannes Steinhoff flew this aircraft with 10.(N)/Jagdgeschwader 26, as Staffelkapitän, while based at Jever in December 1939. The unit was one of the handful of semi-autonomous night-fighter units, nearly all of which applied an 'N' to the left of the fuselage cross insignia.

Following the pre-production Bf 109B-0 with a 455kW (610hp) Jumo 210B engine, the fighter went into full-scale production for the Luftwaffe as the Bf 109B-1, which was powered by a 474kW (635hp) Jumo 210D engine, and the Bf 109B-2, powered by a 477kW (640hp) Jumo 210E; this powerplant was in turn superseded by the Jumo 210G developing 500kW (670hp). Alternative sources suggest that the Bf 109B-1 and B-2 were differentiated by their propeller type – either the Schwarz or VDM model – while others do not identify any subvariants of the B-series.

First production models

The first production Bf 109Bs were delivered to JG 132 'Richthofen' in early 1937. From that summer, the aircraft was engaged in operational trials in the Spanish Civil War. The B-model enjoyed only a relatively brief service career before it was superseded by improved versions

and the last of the 'Berthas' were active with fighter schools in early 1940.

The second production series involved the Bf 109C-1, which introduced the 522kW (700hp) Jumo 210G engine. Such was the success of the fighter that before long Arado, Focke-Wulf and Fieseler were all engaged in its manufacture. By September 1938 almost 600 examples had been completed, and there were more than 1000 in Luftwaffe service by the outbreak of World War II.

The C-model was further differentiated as the Bf 109C-1, C-2 and C-3, all sharing the Jumo 210G engine but with different armament configurations. The C-1 had two nose-mounted MG 17s and another two in the wings. The C-2 would have had a fifth MG 17 mounted in the engine but was not proceeded with. Finally, the C-3 replaced the wing-mounted machine guns with MG FF cannon. Since the Bf 109C was built in parallel

21

with the superior D-model, production of the former remained limited.

In the meantime, the aircraft had demonstrated some of its potential for continued development when five non-standard examples took part in an international flying meet in Zurich, two of them fitted with 708kW (950hp) Daimler-Benz engines.

The resulting performance boost ensured the team won the Circuit of the Alps contest, as well as a team race, speed event and a climb and dive competition.

Speed record

Then, on 11 November 1937, a Bf 109 flown by Hermann Wurster pushed the landplane world speed record to 610.55km/h (379.38mph), this aircraft being equipped with a boosted Daimler-Benz DB 601 with an output of 1230kW (1650hp).

Bf 109D

Once – erroneously – considered to be the first of the line to receive the DB 600 engine, the Bf 109D in fact reverted to the Jumo 210Da, but combined this with a four-gun armament. A batch of five Bf 109Ds was sent to Spain for combat trials and this variant also won export orders from Hungary, which took three examples for evaluation, and Switzerland, which received 10 that were used for pilot familiarization ahead of deliveries of the Bf 109E.

Messerschmitt Bf 109E-4s of Jagdgeschwader 27 (JG 27) are refuelled during the Battle of Britain. JG 27 claimed 146 enemy aircraft shot down, although the unit itself had lost 83 Bf 109Es by December 1940.

Messerschmitt Bf 109E

The first of the Bf 109s to enter large-scale production and service was the Bf 109E, or 'Emil', which finally introduced the promised Daimler-Benz DB 600/601 engine.

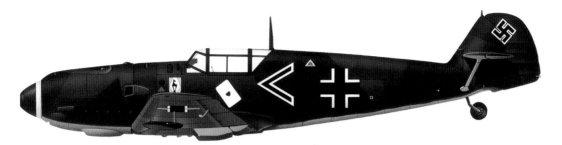

Messerschmitt Bf 109E-1

Weight (Maximum take-off) 2505kg (5523lb)

Dimensions Length: 8.76m (28ft 7in), Wingspan: 9.87m (32ft 4in), Height: 2.28m (7ft 5in)

Powerplant One 864kW (1158hp) DB 601A-1 piston V-12 engine

Speed 570km/h (354mph)

Range 660km (410 miles)

Ceiling 10,500m (34,450ft)

Crew 1

Armament Four 7.92mm (0.31in) MG 17 machine guns (two in wings, two in nose)

Messerschmitt Bf 109E-1

Piloted by *Oberst* Josef 'Pips' Priller, this aircraft was assigned to I./Jagdgeschwader 51 based at Münster Handorf, northwest Germany, in October 1939.

The first Bf 109Es rolled out of the factories in late 1938 and were destined to become perhaps the best-known of this famous line of fighters.

The prototype for the 'Emil' was the V10, the tenth pre-production machine, which was the first to be fitted with the DB 600. The same unit was tested in other prototypes before switching to the DB 601A with more power and fuel injection. The latter feature would be of utmost importance when the Bf 109 went to war, since it ensured the engine could maintain power even under negative G-force, gaining a distinct tactical advantage.

New variant

The combination of DB 601A and Bf 109 was first expressed in the Bf 109E-1 variant, probably the finest fighter in the world at the time of its appearance. The armament of the Bf 109D was retained – two 7.92mm (0.3in) MG 17 machine guns in the upper fuselage

decking and another pair in the wings. Cannon armament was introduced in the Bf 109E-3, which was fitted with a pair of 20mm (0.8in) MG FF cannon in the wings, providing another advantage over Allied fighter opposition in the early years of the war.

Combat experience

The first production deliveries of the Bf 109E-1 and E-3 went to Spain, where an initial batch of 40 arrived in December 1938. These would become the backbone of the Nationalist air force. Additional exports were made to Switzerland and Yugoslavia, while in the first half of 1939 the Luftwaffe quickly began to introduce the new version. With production under way with Messerschmitt, Erla, Fieseler and WNF, more than 1000 examples had been delivered to the Luftwaffe by the outbreak of World War II.

After playing a limited role in the campaigns against Poland and in the invasions of Denmark and Norway, the Bf 109E saw considerable action over the Low Countries and in the Battle of France. During the Battle of Britain, the 'Emil' performed well, especially in the unrestrained *freie Jagd* role, in

which pilots could make the best use of the fighter's excellent dive and climb performance. However, once tactics changed and the Bf 109E was pressed into the bomber escort role, losses began to mount.

The lessons of the early battles were incorporated in the Bf 109E-4 version that was fielded from mid-1940. This had wing-mounted MG FF/M cannon that featured an improved feed mechanism, as well as additional armour protection and a new, heavily framed canopy.

From August, the Luftwaffe received the Bf 109E-7, which could carry a drop tank under the fuselage for an increase in range. The same centreline rack could accommodate a 250kg (551lb) SC 250 bomb and in this

capacity the type was used increasingly in a *Jabo* (fighter-bomber) role during the Battle of Britain. Dedicated *Jabo* versions of the E-series added a B suffix to their designation, for example, the Bf 109E-1/B.

A small number of 'Emils' were completed for a reconnaissance role, adding a camera in the rear fuselage at the expense of the wing cannon (Bf 109E-5) or with the wing guns retained (Bf 109E-6).

New engine

Adding the DB 601N engine with 96-octane fuel for an additional boost in power produced the Bf 109E-4/N, while limited numbers were completed as Bf 109E-8 fighters with uprated DB 601E engines or as Bf 109E-9s – equivalent to the E-8, but outfitted for reconnaissance.

After the Battle of Britain, the Bf 109E continued to see active service on cross-Channel operations against the RAF before the focus switched to

Messerschmitt Bf 109E-3

A Bf 109E-3 operated by 7./Jagdgeschwader 53 'Pik As' ('Ace of Spades'), based at Wiesbaden-Erbenheim in October 1939. The pilot was *Oberleutnant* Wolf-Dietrich Wilcke, *Staffelkapitan* of 7./JG 53.

Messerschmitt Bf 109E-3
Weight (Maximum take-off) 2607kg (5747lb)
Dimensions Length: 8.76m (28ft 7in), Wingspan: 9.89m (32ft 5in), Height: 2.58m (8ft 5in)
Powerplant One 876kW (1175hp) DB 601Aa piston V-12 engine
Speed 552km/h (343mph)
Range 660km (410 miles)
Ceiling 10,500m (34,450ft)
Crew 1
Armament Two 20mm (0.8in) MG FF cannon, two 7.92mm (0.31in) MG 17 machine guns

Messerschmitt Bf 109E-3

The 'black chevron and bars' marking on this Bf 109E-3 denoted the aircraft of *Oberstleutnant* Carl Schumacher, the *Geschwaderkommodore* of Jagdgeschwader 1 based at Jever in spring 1940.

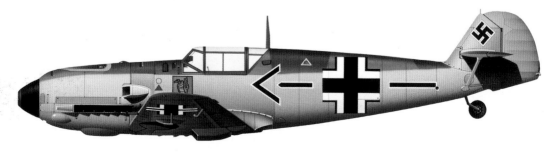

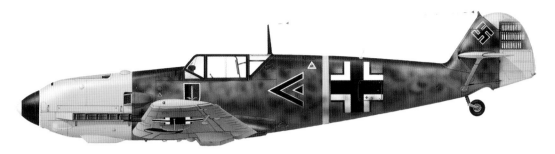

Messerschmitt Bf 109E-4

Weight (Maximum take-off) 2505kg (5523lb)

Dimensions Length: 8.76m (28ft 7in), Wingspan: 9.87m (32ft 4in), Height: 2.28m (7ft 5in)

Powerplant One 894kW (1200hp) DB 601N 12-cylinder inverted-V engine

Speed 570km/h (354mph)

Range 700km (435 miles)

Ceiling 10,500m (34,450ft)

Crew 1

Armament Two 20mm (0.8in) MG FF/M wing cannon, two 7.92mm (0.31in) MG 17 machine guns

Messerschmitt Bf 109E-4

Hauptmann Herbert Ihlefeld flew this Bf 109E-4 while serving as *Gruppenkommandeur* of I.(J)/Lehrgeschwader 2 while based at Molaoi, Greece, during May 1941. Ihlefeld joined I.(J)/LG 2 in 1938 and was *Gruppenkommandeur* from August 1940 to May 1942, by which time the group was designated I./JG 77.

Messerschmitt Bf 109E-4B

This Bf 109E-4B was flown by Lt. Steindl, the *Geschwader-Adjutant* of JG 54 *Grünherz*, in the Leningrad area of the Eastern Front, spring 1942.

A *Schwarm* of Bf 109Es from I./JG 3 cross the English Channel in September 1940. The *Gruppe* was based in Pas-de-Calais at this time.

Messerschmitt Bf 109E-4

A Bf 109E-4, the mount of Hans von Hahn,
Gruppenkommandeur of I. Gruppe, Jagdgeschwader
3, based at Grandvillier, France, in August 1940.
The 'Tatzelwurm' emblem on the cowling was used
throughout I. Gruppe of JG 3.

Nose Machine Guns
The Bf 109E included two 7.92mm
(0.31in) machine guns in the nose,
firing through the propeller blades.

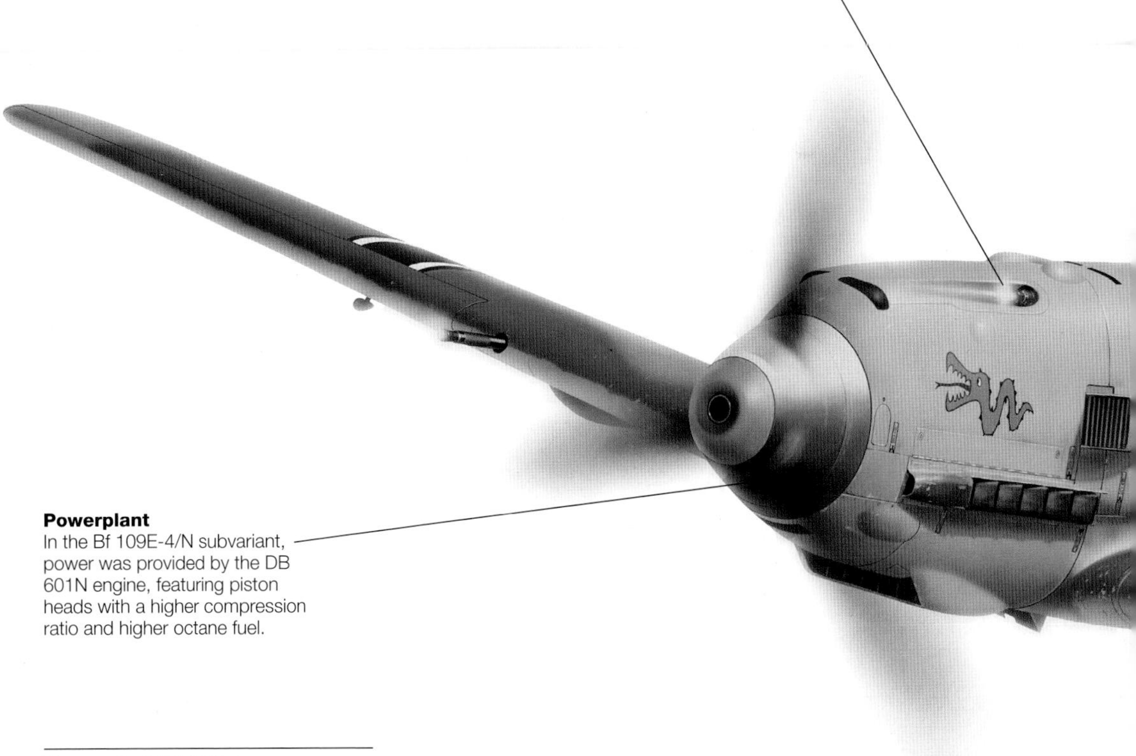

Powerplant
In the Bf 109E-4/N subvariant,
power was provided by the DB
601N engine, featuring piston
heads with a higher compression
ratio and higher octane fuel.

Messerschmitt Bf 109E-4

Weight (Maximum take-off) 2505kg (5523lb)

Dimensions Length: 0.76m (28ft 7in), Wingspan.
9.87m (32ft 4in), Height: 2.28m (7ft 5in)

Powerplant One 894kW (1200hp) DB 601N
12-cylinder inverted-V engine

Speed 570km/h (354mph)

Range 700km (435 miles)

Ceiling 10,500m (34,450ft)

Crew 1

Armament Two 20mm (0.8in) MG FF/M wing
cannon, two 7.92mm (0.31in) MG 17 machine guns

Recognition Markings
In order to ensure that the Bf 109 would be distinguished from enemy fighters in the heat of battle, yellow or white markings began to be applied in August 1940.

Wing Armament
Wing armament for the Bf 109E-4 consisted of two MG FF/M 20mm (0.8in) cannon. This more powerful weapon replaced the two 7.92mm (0.31in) MG 17 machine guns that comprised the original wing firepower.

the Balkans, including the invasion of Yugoslavia. Then, from April 1941, the 'Emil' was heavily engaged in the campaign in North Africa, followed two months later by the invasion of the Soviet Union. Operation 'Barbarossa' was the swansong of the Bf 109E and the type was rapidly superseded by the Bf 109F, most Luftwaffe fighter units converting from the 'Emil' to the subsequent version. However, the Bf 109E remained in use with export operators and survived in Luftwaffe hands in the *Jabo* role until 1943.

Noteworthy is the Bf 109T, a carrier-based development of the Bf 109E-1 intended for service aboard the aircraft carrier *Graf Zeppelin*. Equipped with extended folding wings, a batch of 10 pre-production Bf 109T-0s was completed, but when work on the carrier was abandoned in May 1940, the 60 Bf 109T-1s under production were instead finished as land-based Bf 109T-2s. These saw out their career in Norway and in defence of Heligoland in the North Sea.

Messerschmitt Bf 109E-7

Weight (Maximum take-off) 2505kg (5523lb)
Dimensions Length: 8.76m (28ft 7in), Wingspan: 9.87m (32ft 4in), Height: 2.28m (7ft 5.5in)
Powerplant One 876kW (1175hp) DB 601Aa piston V-12 engine
Speed 570km/h (354mph)
Range 700km (435 miles)
Ceiling 10,500m (34,450ft)
Crew 1
Armament Two 20mm (0.8in) MG FF/M wing cannon, two 7.92mm (0.31in) MG 17 machine guns; one 250kg (551lb) SC 250 bomb

Messerschmitt Bf 109E-7/Trop

Leutnant Werner Schroer flew tropicalized Bf 109E-7 'Black 8' with 8./Jagdgeschwader 27 while based in Libya in April 1941. The upper surfaces painted in sand and green were intended to blend in with the local terrain of sand and camelthorn bushes.

Messerschmitt Bf 109E-7/B

This aircraft was part of Zerstörergeschwader 1 (ZG 1), which operated on the Eastern Front in 1942. The 'C' on the fuselage indicates the unit was part of III Gruppe.

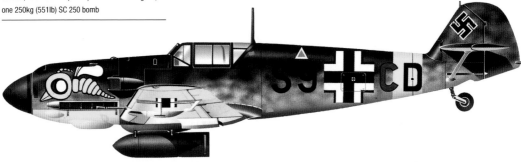

Messerschmitt Bf 109F

The successor to the 'Emil', the Bf 109F was a further development of this aircraft that added progressively uprated versions of the DB 601 engine, together with improved handling via a series of aerodynamic refinements.

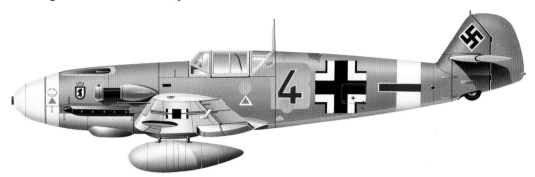

Externally, the 'Friedrich' was identified by its deeper, more streamlined cowling and low-drag radiator, plus a revised wing that allied the structure of the Bf 109E's mainplane with reduced span and new, wider-chord ailerons. The tailwheel was now of the retractable type and the rudder was of reduced size. The previous wing-mounted machine guns were removed in favour of a cannon firing through the engine hub, plus the two machine guns in the upper fuselage decking.

In the course of 1940, four protypes and 10 Bf 109F-0 pre-production aircraft were completed. Although the planned DB 601E and MG 151 cannon were not yet available, the Bf 109F displayed good performance and manoeuvrability with its DB 601N engine and MG FF/M armament inherited from the Bf 109E.

Bf 109F-1 and F-2 models

From October 1940 the initial Bf 109F-1 began to roll off the production lines, now with a new supercharger intake and high-octane fuel. The same month, aircraft began to be issued to the Luftwaffe, and among

the first pilots to receive the type was fighter ace Werner Mölders of Stab/JG 51, then based in France. Despite the Royal Air Force's introduction of the Spitfire Mk V, the 'Friedrich' held its own in terms of dive and climb performance, although it was out-turned by the British fighter.

By March 1941 teething problems had been ironed out and the Bf 109F began to be fielded in quantity by the Luftwaffe. The Bf 109F-2 was delivered alongside the F-1 and differed in its armament of MG 151/15 cannon in place of the MG FF/M. By June 1941, the 'Friedrich' was the primary equipment of the fighter units spearheading the attack on the Soviet Union. The Luftwaffe posted claims of around 1200 Soviet aircraft destroyed on the opening day of Operation 'Barbarossa', and most of these fell to the guns of the Bf 109F.

At the same time, the Bf 109F was re-equipping Luftwaffe fighter units engaged in North Africa, where the type soon supplanted the previous Bf 109E. Desert service prompted new adaptations of the basic aircraft, the Bf 109F-2/Trop and F-4/Trop, featuring

Messerschmitt Bf 109F-2/Trop

Weight (Maximum take-off) 2746kg (6054lb)

Dimensions Length: 8.94m (29ft 4in), Wingspan: 9.92m (32ft 6in), Height: 2.59m (8ft 6in)

Powerplant One 864kW (1159hp) DB 601N 12-cylinder inverted-V engine

Speed 628km/h (390mph)

Range 700km (435 miles)

Ceiling 11,600m (38,000ft)

Crew 2

Armament One 15mm (0.59in) MG 151/15 cannon, two 7.92mm (0.31in) MG 17 machine guns

sand filters. Further subvariants of the F-model were the Bf 109F-2/B that had provision for bomb carriage and the Bf 109F-2/U1 that replaced the 7.92mm (0.31in) MG 17 machine guns with 13mm (0.51in) MG 131s.

Definitive Bf 109F-4

By the end of 1941 the low-octane-fuel DB 601E engine was available and equipped the Bf 109F-3, a short production run of which was followed by the definitive Bf 109F-4. This version introduced the long-awaited 20mm (0.8in) MG 151/20 cannon, together with self-sealing tanks, additional armour and a strengthened tail. While the Bf 109F-4 only saw limited service as a fighter over the English Channel, it found its niche as a fighter-bomber, for which role the Bf 109F-4/B *Jabo* version was made available, making its mark in attacks on British shipping and coastal targets during 1942.

Leutnant Jürgen Harder's Bf 109F-2 is seen on the opening day of Operation 'Barbarossa', June 1941. He was serving with III./JG 53 at the time.

Messerschmitt Bf 109F-2/B

Ship 'kill' markings are worn on the rudder of this Bf 109F-2/B, flown by the *Staffelkapitän* of 10./Jagdgeschwader 2. In 1941–42, a mere 30 Luftwaffe fighters carrying 250kg (551lb) bombs caused severe losses to British shipping in the English Channel.

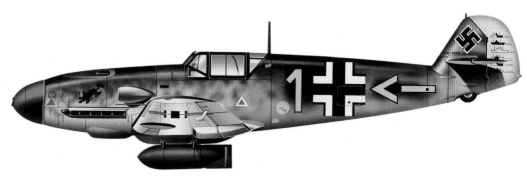

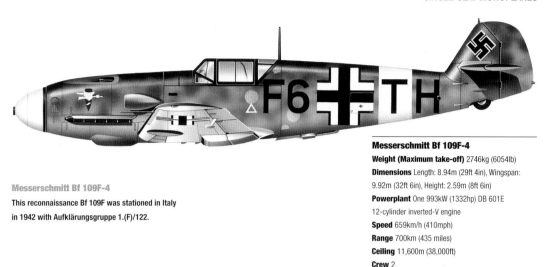

Messerschmitt Bf 109F-4
Weight (Maximum take-off) 2746kg (6054lb)
Dimensions Length: 8.94m (29ft 4in), Wingspan: 9.92m (32ft 6in), Height: 2.59m (8ft 6in)
Powerplant One 993kW (1332hp) DB 601E 12-cylinder inverted-V engine
Speed 659km/h (410mph)
Range 700km (435 miles)
Ceiling 11,600m (38,000ft)
Crew 2
Armament One 20mm (0.8in) MG 151/20 cannon, two 7.92mm (0.31in) MG 17 machine guns

Messerschmitt Bf 109G

It's arguable that the Bf 109F represented the zenith of the Messerschmitt fighter design, but without an adequate, all-new successor, work continued to refine the basic configuration.

Development of the next-generation fighter, the Bf 109G, was under way as of mid-1941 and this would eventually become the most numerous version of the type. The G-model was an effort to wring out yet more performance from the 'Friedrich', improving that version's speed, while handling and manoeuvrability were judged less critical. In order to fight at higher altitudes, the new aircraft would make use of a more powerful DB 605 engine, and a pressurized cockpit was also planned.

Developing 1100kW (1475hp) at take-off, the DB 605 was a progression of the DB 601E, but its increased weight demanded stronger engine bearers and fuselage structure, as well as beefed-up undercarriage.

The first three prototypes began to take shape at Regensburg in October 1941 but at this stage the DB 605 was still not ready. Instead, the Bf 109G-0s were powered by the DB 601E but they incorporated the new cowling.

By the time the first series-production Bf 109G-1s were completed in late spring 1942, the powerplant had switched to the planned DB 605. Otherwise similar, the Bf 109G-2 was built in parallel but without the pressurization equipment. The latter version was produced in greater numbers, but differentiating the two subvariants is hampered by the fact that many of the Bf 109G-2s were completed with the air scoops associated with the pressurization system. The Bf

109G-2 made its debut in the Russian campaign in June 1942.

Bf 109G-4

Next of the 'Gustav' line to enter production was the Bf 109G-4 in October 1942. This model was also unpressurized but introduced minor changes in terms of radio equipment – externally, this was manifest in a different antenna arrangement. Before long, the Bf 109G-4 also added revised landing gear, with larger mainwheels that resulted in characteristic bulges on the upper surfaces of the wings. The Bf 109G-4 was also adapted for reconnaissance missions, some of these receiving water-methanol boosting as the Bf 109G-4/U3. For long-range

Messerschmitt Bf 109G-2

Weight (Maximum take-off) 3400kg (7496lb)

Dimensions Length: 8.95m (29ft 4in), Wingspan: 9.9m (32ft 7in), Height: 2.6m (8ft 6in)

Powerplant One 895kW (1200hp) DB 605A piston V-12 engine

Speed 640km/h (400mph) at 6,300m (20,669ft)

Range 850km (530 miles)

Ceiling 11,600m (38,500ft)

Crew 1

Armament Two 20mm (0.8in) MG 151/20 wing cannon, two 7.92mm (0.31in) MG 17 machine guns

Messerschmitt Bf 109G-2

A Bf-109-2 of 4./JG 54 'Grünherz', Siverskaya, northern sector of the Eastern Front, summer 1942. Note the Vienna-Aspern coat-of-arms ahead of the windscreen. The horizontal bar on the fuselage signifies II Gruppe.

Messerschmitt Bf 109G-6

Assigned to I./Jagdgeschwader 3, this 'Gustav' wears the JG 3 'Udet' badge on the nose and has a grey-and-black spiralled spinner. This *Gruppe* was recalled from the Russian Front in June 1943 for the defence of the Reich, seeing service first in the Netherlands and later within 1. Jagddivision.

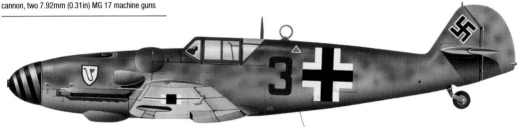

reconnaissance, the Luftwaffe was provided with the Bf 109G-4/R3 that was equipped with a pair of underwing drop tanks plus a camera in the rear fuselage; the 7.92mm (0.31in) MG 17 machine guns were deleted.

Arriving in service after the Bf 109G-4 was the G-3, appearing in March 1943. This was a pressurized high-altitude fighter that incorporated the improvements of the G-3. Only 50 were completed.

Main model

Numerically the most important of the G-series was the Bf 109G-6, over 12,000 examples of which were built.

This variant was intended to be easily adapted for a range of missions and to add new and improved equipment as it became available. Armament was initially based around the existing MG 151/20 cannon, but the MG 17s were replaced by 13mm (0.51in) MG 131s, with 300 rather than 500 rounds per gun. Subsequently, the MG 151/20 began to give way to a 30mm (1.18in) MK 108 cannon, leading to a U4 suffix being added to the designation.

The G-6 entered service in September 1943 and most served in a homeland defence role or otherwise with Luftwaffe units on the Western Front. Some of these aircraft were

Messerschmitt Bf 109G-6

Weight (Maximum take-off) 3400kg (7496lb)

Dimensions Length: 8.95m (29ft 4in), Wingspan: 9.9m (32ft 7in), Height: 2.6m (8ft 6in)

Powerplant One 895kW (1200hp) DB 605A piston V-12 engine

Speed 640km/h (400mph) at 6300m (20,669ft)

Range 850km (530 miles)

Ceiling 12,000m (39,000ft)

Crew 1

Armament Two 20mm (0.8in) MG 151/20 wing cannon, two 13mm (0.51in) MG 131 machine guns; one 250kg (551lb) bomb or four 50kg (110lb) bombs or one 300-litre (66 Imp gal) drop tank

completed as Bf 109G-5s – the same as the G-6 but with the pressurization system reinstated. A wide variety of conversion kits were supplied to adapt the basic Bf 109G-6, including water-methanol boost (adding a U2 or U3 suffix to the designation). Meanwhile, the U5 was armed with an MG 151/20 but carried a pair of MK 108 cannon in underwing gondolas, while the U6 was fitted with three MK 108s.

As well as the various U designations, smaller equipment changes were incorporated in *Rüstsätze* – modifications that could be made to the Bf 109G-6 in the field. As well as the R2 and R3 for reconnaissance (with equipment similar to the Bf 109G-4), there was the R1 for a centreline bomb rack, and the R6 that added underwing MG 151/20s. Another option for the G6 was the Werfergranate 21, a 210mm (8.75in)

mortar that was launched against enemy bomber formations from a pair of underwing tubes.

While the water-methanol boost provided an improvement in performance, a more significant change was the adoption of the DB 605A engine with additional supercharging for an output of 895kW (1200hp). A redesigned engine cowling was required to accommodate the larger supercharger, leading to a more streamlined appearance.

Fielded from spring 1944, the DB 605A-engined version was the Bf 109G-6/AS. The additional performance was useful for the defence of the Reich mission, and examples of the Bf 109G-6/AS were also produced through conversion of existing airframes. Some of these variants also served with night fighter units.

Bf 109Gs were often fitted with *Rüstsätze*-1 kit, which added an extra bomb rack for a single 500kg (1102lb) bomb on the centreline. This Bf 109G-6 served with JG 3.

Messerschmitt Bf 109G-10

Weight (Maximum take-off) 3400kg (7496lb)

Dimensions Length: 8.95m (29ft 4in), Wingspan: 9.9m (32ft 7in), Height: 2.6m (8ft 6in)

Powerplant One 1250kW (1677hp) DB 605D-2 piston V-12 engine

Speed 640km/h (400mph) at 6300m (20,669ft)

Range 850km (530 miles)

Ceiling 12,000m (39,000ft)

Crew 1

Armament Two 20mm (0.8in) MG 151/20 wing cannon, two 13mm (0.51in) MG 131 machine guns

Messerschmitt Bf 109K

By the time production of the Bf 109G was in full swing, the plethora of different subvariants, conversion kits and equipment changes provided Luftwaffe ground crews with a logistical nightmare.

In a final attempt to rationalize the production programme, Messerschmitt introduced the Bf 109K, based around the latest DB 605DM engine, rated at 1492kW (2000hp) for take-off. While the Bf 109K boasted plenty of speed, it was not as fine in terms of handling as its predecessors, but it was above all hampered by the shortages of experienced pilots and fuel that afflicted the Luftwaffe in the closing stages of the war.

Bf 109K-4

After a small batch of pre-production Bf 109K-0s with water-methanol-boosted DB 605DMs, plans to produce three separate Bf 109K-1 (with pressurization), K-2 (standard fighter) and K-3 (reconnaissance fighter) variants were abandoned in favour

of further rationalization. The result was the Bf 109K-4, which was the only version of the 'Kurfürst' to enter quantity production, the first examples coming off the production lines in summer 1944. The initial units to field the new fighter were III./JG 27 and III./JG 77, and the type was first noted in action in November 1944, when examples clashed with Allied bombers and their escort fighters near Leipzig.

Key features of the Bf 109K-4 were the DB 605DM engine with bulged cowling, tail fin, long tailwheel, deep oil cooler, wide-blade propeller, rectangular wing fairings for the larger mainwheels and a radio antenna below the port wing. Standard cannon armament was the MK 108. While all these features were found on some of the later-model Bf 109Gs, unique

to the Bf 109K-4 were the relocated ADF loop antenna (moved further back on the spine), aileron trim tabs and additional undercarriage doors to cover the lower portions of the mainwheels.

Rüstsätze modification kits

As was the case for the G-series, a number of *Rüstsätze* modification kits were available to be implemented by ground crew. Among these were provision for bomb carriage (R1), reconnaissance (R2), drop tank (R3), underwing cannon (R4) and gun camera in the port wing (R6). In the confusion of the final months of the war in Europe there emerged a Bf 109K-6 heavy fighter development, tested in late 1944, but apparently never destined for production.

Other subvariants mentioned include the Bf 109K-8 reconnaissance fighter, the Bf 109K-10 with MK 103M engine cannon and the Bf 109K-14 high-altitude fighter; but it seems few, if any, of these were actually fielded by the Luftwaffe. Another abortive development was a two-seat trainer version – the Bf 109K-12.

It's also worth mentioning the last of the 'Gustavs' – the Bf 109G-10 – introduced in an effort to bring older G-models up to the same standard as the definitive Bf 109K-4. Since this was not always entirely practical, the resulting Bf 109G-10s were completed to a variety of different standards. Nevertheless, together with the Bf

109K-4, the G-10 became the most important variant of the fighter in the final months of the war, with around 2600 upgrades being completed. Ultimately, it seems that few if any Luftwaffe units exclusively flew the Bf 109K-4, and most operated this version alongside the G-series.

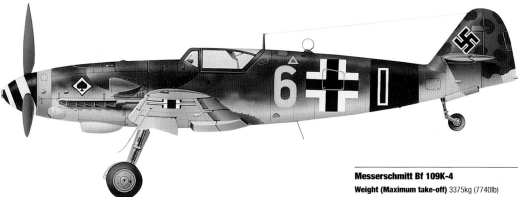

Messerschmitt Bf 109K-4

The Bf 109K-4 was the last variant to be built in any quantity, reaching the front line in October 1944. This aircraft flew with III./JG 53 and was based at Kirrlach in Bavaria in March 1945.

Messerschmitt Bf 109K-4

This aircraft flew with II./JG 77 at Bönninghardt, December 1944.

Messerschmitt Bf 109K-4
Weight (Maximum take-off) 3375kg (7740lb)
Dimensions Length: 9.04m (29ft 8in), Wingspan: 9.92m (32ft 6in), Height: 2.59m (8ft 6in)
Powerplant One 1492kW (2000hp) DB 605DM engine
Speed 710km/h (440mph)
Range 700km (435 miles)
Ceiling 12,500m (41,000ft)
Crew 1
Armament One 30mm (1.18in) MK 108 engine-mounted cannon, two 13mm (0.51in) MG 131 machine guns

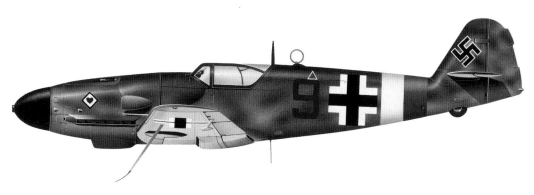

Focke-Wulf Fw 190 prototypes

The Fw 190 began life in 1937 as work started to provide a successor to the first generation of monoplane fighters. Compared to its predecessors, the new design was intended to offer improved performance, high structural integrity and ease of maintenance under combat conditions.

Designed by Kurt Tank, the Fw 190 was drafted with two alternative powerplants: an inline Daimler-Benz DB 601 or the 18-cylinder radial BMW 139. Since the radial offered more power – 1156kW (1550hp) was achieved in bench tests – as well as superior resistance to battle damage, this was the unit selected for the first prototype. After the Luftwaffe's technical office gave its support to Tank's design in summer 1938, construction of three prototypes commenced. By the following spring a fourth aircraft had been added to the prototype batch, which was by now taking shape at Bremen, and a pre-

production batch of 40 more aircraft was planned.

First prototype

The first prototype, Fw 190 V1, took to the air at Bremen on 1 June 1939, with Hans Sander at the controls. Despite overheating of the engine, the test pilot was full of praise for the new aircraft, reporting that, 'The controls were light, positive and well balanced.' The second prototype, V2, followed it into the air in October, and this was the first to carry armament, in the form of a single 7.92mm (0.31in) MG 17 machine gun in each wing root. In early trials at Rechlin the Fw

By early 1940, the Fw 190 V1 prototype had a conventional propeller and spinner and was coded FO+LY.

190 prototypes demonstrated a top speed of 594km/h (369mph) – clearly superior to the Bf 109.

The first two prototypes were fitted with large, low-drag ducted spinners, but were otherwise conventional with a low-mounted monoplane, retractable tailwheel undercarriage and tractor airscrew. Salient features included a frameless bubble canopy affording the pilot excellent all-round vision. Also ahead of its time was the use of rigid rods to operate the control surfaces, overcoming the problems associated with systems based on wires, pulleys and cranks.

The unusual ducted spinner was soon discarded after problems with overheating continued, and the BMW 139 was also dropped in favour of the BMW 801, a 14-cylinder radial with fan-assisted cooling. While the new engine was of the same dimensions as the BMW 139, it offered an additional 112kW (150hp) of power.

On the other hand, the new unit was also heavier, by around 635kg (1400lb), necessitating a redesign of the Fw 190's forward fuselage and restressing of the airframe. While the test programme continued using the BMW 139-powered Fw 190 V1 and V2, the third and fourth prototypes were cancelled.

Fw 190 V5

The first prototype with the BMW 801 was Fw 190 V5, which joined the flight-test programme in April 1940. The additional weight of the engine had an adverse effect on handling and demanded an increased-area wing – boosting the surface from 15m² (161.46 sq ft) to 18.3m² (197 sq ft). After being fitted with new wing and tail surfaces, Fw 190 V5 resumed flight trials in summer 1940. It was decided that all aircraft on the production line would be completed with the same wing.

Fw 190 V5, the fifth aircraft, was the first to be fitted with a BMW 801 engine, necessitating the enlargement of its wings.

These Focke-Wulf Fw 190Fs from II Gruppe, Schlachtgeschwader 1, have bomb racks fitted.

Focke-Wulf Fw 190A

The first examples of the 40 pre-production Fw 190A-0s were completed at Bremen in autumn 1940. Before long, factories of the Arado and AGO companies would join the production effort.

The first six pre-production Fw 190A-0s were delivered to a dedicated test unit, the Erprobungsstaffel 190 based at Rechlin, in March 1941. Crews for the new unit were drawn from the II. Gruppe of Jagdgeschwader 26 and they soon encountered some problems with their new equipment. Like the previous BMW 139, the BMW 801 powerplant was prone to overheating and the automatic fuel control system was troublesome.

These issues were eventually ironed out and by June 1941 the production-standard Fw 190A-1 had begun to leave the Bremen factory, powered by the 1238kW (1660hp) BMW 801C-1 engine, followed soon after by the first

such aircraft completed by Arado and AGO. A total of 82 Fw 190A-1 fighters had been delivered to the Luftwaffe by the end of September 1941 and additional units within JG 26 began to receive the new fighter, among them II./JG 26 based at Moorseele in Belgium and III./JG 26 at Liegescourt in northern France.

While deficiencies in the automatic fuel control system were quickly rectified, overheating remained a problem even after the Fw 190A-1 had gone into combat, in some cases leading to in-flight fires. The armament of the initial series-production version was also clearly deficient: just four 7.92mm (0.31in) MG 17 machine guns.

Despite these setbacks, the fighter quickly proved itself superior to the Royal Air Force's Spitfire Mk V.

By autumn 1941 the initial-production Fw 190A-1 variant had been superseded by the Fw 190A-2, which introduced an improved BMW 801C-2 engine and replaced the two wing-root MG 17 machine guns with 20mm (0.8in) MG FF cannon; the two MG 17s mounted above the engine were retained and on some aircraft firepower was further boosted by another pair of MG 17s in the outer wing panels.

In a bid to improve the fighter's ability to tackle bomber targets, some Fw 190A-1s and A-2s were up-armed

with two additional 20mm (0.8in) MG/FF cannon in the wings.

By the end of 1941 the Luftwaffe had taken more than 200 Fw 190As on charge and early the following year it began to receive the next subvariant, the Fw 190A-3. This model introduced another new engine, the BMW 801Dg, providing 1342kW (1800hp) at take-off. By this point, the fighter's armament had also been standardized on four cannon and two machine guns: the MG FF cannon were moved to the outer wing panels and their original locations received faster-firing 20mm (0.8in) MG 151 weapons. This same 'fit' was retrospectively introduced on surviving Fw 190A-1s and A-2s.

Other refinements were introduced to the Fw 190A-3 during its production run, including improved radios. Among the subvariants of the Fw 190A-3 were the Fw 190A-3/U1 and Fw 190A-3/U3 for close support duties and the Fw 190A-3/U4 reconnaissance fighter. The recce version typically had the

outboard MG FF cannon removed and camera and/or bomb racks added.

As of late spring 1942 there were around 260 Fw 190s equipping JG 2 and JG 26 and teething problems had been addressed. A temporary ban on overwater operations introduced as a result of engine overheating concerns was lifted, allowing the fighter to go on the offensive over the English Channel.

A dramatic demonstration of the Fw 190's prowess came when examples from I. and III./JG 26 clashed with

Focke-Wulf 190A-3
Weight (Maximum take-off) 4900kg (10,800lb)
Dimensions Length: 8.84m (29ft), Wingspan: 10.50m (34ft 5in), Height: 3.96m (13ft)
Powerplant One 1342kW (1800hp) BMW 801Dg piston radial engine
Speed 605km/h (375mph)
Range 800km (500 miles)
Ceiling 10,600m (34,776ft)
Crew 1
Armament Four 20mm (0.8in) MG 151 and MG FF cannon, two 7.92mm (0.31in) machine guns

Focke-Wulf Fw 190A-3
Hauptmann Herbert Wehnelt flew this Fw 190A-3 as *Staffelkapitän* of 7./Jagdgeschwader 51, based at Orel around January 1943.

Focke-Wulf 190A-4
Weight (Maximum take-off) 4900kg (10,800lb)
Dimensions Length: 8.84m (29ft), Wingspan: 10.50m (34ft 5in), Height: 3.96m (13ft)
Powerplant One 1566kW (2100hp) BMW 801D-2 radial engine
Speed 670km/h (416mph)
Range 800km (500 miles)
Ceiling 10,600m (34,776ft)
Crew 1
Armament Four 20mm (0.8in) MG 151 and MG FF cannon, two 7.92mm (0.31in) machine guns

Focke-Wulf Fw 190A-4
Major Hubertus von Bonin flew Fw 190A-4 while serving as commander of Jagdgeschwader 54. The aircraft was operating from Krasnogvardeysky in August 1943.

Focke-Wulf Fw 190A-5

Piloted by *Oberleutnant* Walter Nowotny, among others, this Fw 190A-5 was part of 1./ Jagdgeschwader 54. The bulk of Nowotny's 258 victories were gained in the Focke-Wulf.

seven squadrons of RAF Spitfire Mk Vs that were escorting bomb-carrying Hurricanes on a Circus operation on 1 June 1942. Using radar to aid them, 40 Fw 190s attacked the raiders as they headed for their target in Belgium. In the process, eight Spitfires quickly fell to the German fighters' guns and another five were battle-damaged and forced to return to base. None of the Fw 190s suffered damage.

The Fw 190A-4 was delivered from summer 1942 with a revised radio fit, including a fin-mounted radio

Focke-Wulf Fw 190A-6

This aircraft was flown by *Leutnant* Emil Lang, who served with 5./Jagdgeschwader 54 'Grünherz' ('Green Hearts'). The aircraft was operated on the Eastern Front in October 1943.

mast. The BMW 801D-2 engine had provision for water-methanol boost to provide 1566kW (2100hp) for short periods, increasing top speed to 670km/h (416mph) at 6400m (21,000ft). The Fw 190A-4/Trop was tailored for Mediterranean service with dust filters and provision for a 250kg (551lb) bomb under the fuselage.

Another derivative was the Fw 190A-4/R6 that had no provision for water/methanol boost but added a pair of 210mm (8.75in) Werfergranate 21 mortar tubes under the wings.

The Fw 190A-4/U5, meanwhile, could carry a drop tank below each wing as well as a 500kg (1102lb) bomb below the fuselage.

The Fw 190A-3 and A-4 served as the basis for fighter-bomber experiments conducted against targets on the south coast of England in summer 1942. For the *Jabo* role, the Fw 190As lost their outer wing guns and instead received a bomb rack below the fuselage. Weapons options

Focke-Wulf 190A-5

Weight (Maximum take-off) 4900kg (10,800lb)
Dimensions Length: 8.84m (29ft), Wingspan: 10.50m (34ft 5in), Height: 3.96m (13ft)
Powerplant One 1267kW (1700hp) BMW 801D-2 piston engine
Speed 654km/h (408mph)
Range 800km (500 miles)
Ceiling 10,600m (34,776ft)
Crew 1
Armament Four 20mm (0.8in) MG 151 and MG FF cannon, two 7.92mm (0.31in) machine guns

Focke-Wulf 190A-6

Weight (Maximum take-off) 4900kg (10,800lb)
Dimensions Length: 8.84m (29ft), Wingspan: 10.50m (34ft 5in), Height: 3.96m (13ft)
Powerplant One 1267kW (1700hp) BMW 801D-2 piston engine
Speed 654km/h (408mph)
Range 800km (500 miles)
Ceiling 10,600m (34,776ft)
Crew 1
Armament Two 7.92mm (0.31in) MG 17 machine guns, four 20mm (0.8in) MG 151/20 cannon

were the 250kg (551lb) SC 250 and the 500kg (1102lb) SC 500 bomb.

Next in line among the A-series was the Fw 190A-5 that appeared in spring 1943 with the engine mounting lengthened slightly to provide improved handling. The Fw 190A-5 proved to be especially adaptable, examples being completed as the Fw 190A-5/U2 with flame-dampeners for night operations, two MG 151/20 cannon, under-fuselage bomb rack and provision for underwing drop tanks. The similar Fw 190A-5/U3 could be armed with a 500kg (1102lb) bomb below the fuselage and a pair of 115kg (254lb) bombs below the wings. A reconnaissance version, the Fw 190A-5/U4, carried a pair of cameras.

Among the fighter-bomber derivatives were the Fw 190A-5/U6 and the long-range Fw 190A-5/U7, while the Fw 190A-5/U11 was fitted with a 30mm (1.18in) MK 103 cannon under each wing for the close support role. The Fw 190A-5/U12 combined two MG 151/20 cannon and two MG 17s with a pair of WB 151A pods each armed with a pair of MG 151/20s. For anti-shipping operations, the Fw 190A-5/U14 and U15 could carry a single torpedo each. Finally, the Fw 190A-5/U11 introduced a 30mm (1.18in) MK 108 cannon in the outboard wing positions.

The A-5 soon gave way to a further improved model, the Fw 190A-6 of June 1943 that featured additional armour and four faster-firing 20mm (0.8in) MG 151/20 cannon in the outer positions within a lightened wing. Still heavier armament was available in the Fw 190A-6/R1, with no fewer than six MG 151/20s; the Fw 190A-6/R2 with a 30mm (1.18in) MK 108 in the outboard

Focke-Wulf Fw 190A-8

Hauptmann Paul-Heinrich Dähne flew this aircraft when he was *Gruppenkommandeur* of II./ Jagdgeschwader 1, based in Mecklenburg around February 1945.

Focke-Wulf 190A-8

Weight (Maximum take-off) 4900kg (10,800lb)
Dimensions Length: 8.95m (29ft 4in), Wingspan: 10.50m (34ft 5in), Height: 3.96m (13ft)
Powerplant One 1567kW (2100hp) BMW 801D-2 14 cylinder radial piston engine
Speed 654km/h (408mph)
Range 805km (500 miles)
Ceiling 11,400m (37,400ft)
Crew 1
Armament Two 7.92mm (0.31in) MG 17 machine guns, four 20mm (0.8in) MG 151/20 cannon; one 500kg (1100lb) and two 250kg (550lb) bombs

Focke-Wulf Fw 190A-8
Wearing the markings of 1./Jagdgeschwader 54, 'White 12' was the mount of pilot *Oberleutnant* Josef Heinzeller, based at Schrunden in December 1944. An ace with 35 victories, Heinzeller was head of JG 54's 1. Staffel.

wing positions; the Fw 190A-6/R3 with two 30mm (1.18in) MK 103s under the wings; and the Fw 190A-6/R6 with the Werfergranate 21 tubes.

Towards the end of 1943 the Fw 190A-7 appeared, substituting a pair of 13mm (0.51in) MG 131 heavy machine guns for the MG 17 weapons mounted above the engine. It was otherwise similar to the Fw 190A-6.

The ultimate A-series fighter was the Fw 190A-8 and this would prove to be numerically the most important. It featured a number of detail improvements over the Fw 190A-7, including an additional 114 litres (25 Imp gal) of fuel and was equipped

Focke-Wulf Fw 190A-9

Hauptmann Helmut Wettstein flew this bulged-canopy Fw 190A-9 while assigned to 6./ Jagdgeschwader 54. The fighter was based at Libau-Nord, Latvia, in February 1945. The former boss of 1./JG 54, Wettstein ended the war as commander of 6./JG 54.

Focke-Wulf Fw 190A-8

Named 'Tanja', this Fw 190A-8 was flown by *Leutnant* Gunther Heym of the Stab./ Jagdgeschwader 51. It was based at Zichenau in September 1944.

to accommodate a wider range of field modifications. In addition to subvariants similar to those in the Fw 190A-6 series, the A-8 yielded the Fw 190A-8/R7 with armoured cockpit, Fw 190A-8/R11 all-weather fighter, Fw 190A-8/U1 two-seat conversion trainer and the Fw 190A-8/U3, which was the director component of the Fw 190/Ta 154 Mistel composite aircraft.

In an effort to improve the high-altitude performance of the fighter, Focke-Wulf began work on the Fw 190B. This commenced with modifications to three existing Fw 190A-0 aircraft: the Fw 190 V13 that featured an increased-area wing, pressurized cockpit and boosted BMW 801D-2 engine; and the Fw 190 V16

and V18 that were similar, but with standard wing and armament of two MG 17s and two MG 151/20 cannon. The original radial engine was then replaced by a Daimler-Benz DB 603 inverted-Vee with annular radiator. However, the B-series was abandoned in favour of the Fw 190C – itself destined to be a developmental step on the path to the 'long-nose' Fw 190D.

Focke-Wulf 190A-9

Weight (Maximum take-off) 4900kg (10,800lb)
Dimensions Length: 8.95m (29ft 4in), Wingspan: 10.50m (34ft 5in), Height: 3.96m (13ft)
Powerplant One 1471kW (1973hp) BMW 801S piston radial piston engine
Speed 654km/h (408mph)
Range 805km (500 miles)
Ceiling 11,400m (37,400ft)
Crew 1
Armament Two 7.92mm (0.31in) MG 17 machine guns, four 20mm (0.8in) MG 151/20 cannon; one 500kg (1100lb) and two 250kg (550lb) bombs

Focke-Wulf Fw 190C/D

Following trials of the Daimler-Benz DB 603 inverted-Vee engine in the Fw 190B prototypes, work focused on the Fw 190C – the second high-altitude version of the basic design.

This resulted in a batch of development aircraft powered by the 1304kW (1750hp) DB 603 inline engine cooled by an annular radiator, driving a four-bladed propeller and boosted by either a DVL or a Hirth turbocharger. The installation of the turbocharger unit in a large ventral fairing led to the nickname 'Kanguruh'.

Development of the C-series was abandoned in early 1944 in favour of the medium-level Fw 190D, which began life in late 1943 when several Fw 190A-7s were modified with a 1320kW (1770hp) Jumo 213A-1 inverted-Vee engine with an annular radiator. These Fw 190D-0 prototypes featured an additional 60cm (2ft) 'stretch' to the nose, compensated by an extended rear fuselage – in the form of a 20cm (7.75in) 'plug' – and a tailfin of increased area. Armament remained four MG 151 cannon in the wings and two MG 17 machine guns in the fuselage upper decking.

Fw 190D-9

Armament for the production Fw 190D-9 (the numerical designation was chosen since it followed the Fw 190A-8 on the production line) was a pair of wing-mounted MG 151/20 cannon and two MG 131 machine guns above the engine. There was provision for a drop tank under each wing or a 250kg (551lb) bomb on the under-fuselage station. With additional water-methanol boost, the Fw 190D-9 could produce an emergency power output of 1670kW (2240hp). The Fw 190D-9 also had a broader fin compared to the Fw 190D-0.

First flown at Langenhagen in May 1944, the Fw 190D-9 received production approval around mid-June 1944 and the first examples were delivered to III./JG 54 in September, and were charged with defence of the jet base of *Kommando Nowotny*, flying the Messerschmitt Me 262. Next recipient of the 'Dora-9' was I./JG 26.

Fw 190D-10

Just two Fw 190D-9s were converted to Fw 190D-10 standard with the Jumo 213C engine and a 30mm (1.18in) MK 108 cannon installed to fire through the propeller hub instead of the two MG 131 machine guns.

The Fw 190D-11 did not progress beyond the prototype stage, but the seven examples that were completed

---

Focke-Wulf 190D-9

Weight (Maximum take-off) 4840kg (10,670lb)

Dimensions Length: 10.19m (33ft 5in), Wingspan: 10.50m (34ft 5in), Height: 3.36m (11ft)

Powerplant One 1320kW (1770hp) Junkers Jumo 213A-1 12-cylinder inverted-V piston engine

Speed 686km/h (426mph)

Range 837km (520 miles)

Ceiling 10,000m (32,800ft)

Crew 1

Armament Two 20mm (0.8in) MG 151/20 cannon, two 13mm (0.51in) MG 131 machine guns; provision for one 500kg (1100lb) SC 500 bomb

---

Although originally regarded as a stop-gap until the Ta 152 was developed, the Fw 190D proved to be one of the best Luftwaffe fighters of the war.

featured the Jumo 213E engine, two MG 151/20 cannon in the wing roots and two MK 108 cannon further outboard in the wing.

Fw 190D-12

In an effort to produce a dedicated ground-attack version of the 'Dora', Focke-Wulf produced the Fw 190D-12, which featured the engine-mounted MK 108 and the two MG 151/20 cannon in the wing, but which added extra armour protection for the engine. The Fw 190D-13 was similar to the D-12 but with an

MG 151/20 machine gun in place of the MK 108 cannon. The Fw 190D-14 and D-15 would have been, respectively, a new-build fighter with DB 603 engine and a conversion of the Fw 190A-8 with the same powerplant.

In the event, only the Fw 190D-9 saw combat and examples of this variant equipped most of the Luftwaffe day fighter units in the final months of the war in Europe. Despite their quality, they were frequently overwhelmed by the numerical superiority enjoyed by the Allied fighters by this time.

Focke-Wulf Fw 190D-9

With the *Werknummer* 210079 worn on the top of the tail fin, Fw 190D-9 'Black 12' was assigned to 10./Jagdgeschwader 54 in Belgium in early 1945 and flown by *Leutnant* Theo Nibel. It took part in Operation 'Bodenplatte' in January 1945.

Focke-Wulf Fw 190F

With the Junkers Ju 87 proving increasingly vulnerable in its original close support role from summer 1942, work began on a development of the Fw 190 to be fielded by the *Schlachtgeschwader* (ground-attack wings).

As an interim measure, the Luftwaffe received bombs racks for some of the existing fighter variants, the Fw 190A-4 and A-5 typically receiving a rack below the fuselage to carry a bombload of up to 500kg (1102lb). While this offered better survivability against Allied fighters, the weight of anti-aircraft fire on the Eastern Front in particular demanded a tailor-made solution. The 'fighter' Fw 190 featured some armour for the pilot, but this was arranged to protect him against rounds coming from either ahead or behind.

Ground-attack fighter

In response, the Luftwaffe drafted a requirement for a ground-attack Fw 190, with armour suitable for the role. The resulting Fw 190F included armour plating and laminated glass to protect the pilot against projectiles coming from anywhere in the lower hemisphere.

The armour comprised curved steel sheets of 5mm (0.2in) thickness along either side of the cockpit, and the underside of the fuselage, stretching from the front of the engine cowling

to behind the cockpit. To compensate for the additional weight, the two outer-wing 20mm (0.8in) cannon were removed entirely.

The first examples of the Fw 190F were delivered towards the end of 1942 and the variant proved to be an immediate success, bring much-needed protection to the pilot against ground fire while also retaining the ability to tackle enemy fighters if they became engaged in aerial combat.

Armament

In combat the Fw 190F employed its two 13mm (0.51in) and two 20mm (0.8in) guns for strafing attacks.

Meanwhile, disposable stores could include 250kg (551lb) SC 250 and 500kg (1102lb) SC 500 bombs on a centreline bomb rack as well as containers carrying SD 2, SD 4 and SD 10 bomblets. These sub-munitions could be carried in an AB 250 cluster bomb, each of which could deliver up to 144 SD 2 'butterfly bombs', 30 of the larger SD 4 weapons, or 17 of the still-larger SD 10 sub-munitions. Other options included a single SC

Flown by *Oberleutnant* Karl Kennel, this Fw 190F-2 was on the strength of Schlachtgeschwader 1.

Focke-Wulf 190F-2

Weight (Maximum take-off) 4900kg (10,800lb)

Dimensions Length: 8.84m (29ft), Wingspan: 10.49m (34ft 5in), Height: 3.96m (13ft)

Powerplant One 1268kW (1700hp) BMW 801D-2 18-cylinder two row radial

Speed 653km/h (408mph)

Range 900km (560 miles)

Ceiling 11,410m (37,400ft)

Crew 1

Armament Two 20mm (0.8in) MG 151/20 cannon; two 7.92mm (0.3in) machine guns; two 1800kg (3968lb) bombs

---

250 on the centreline plus four 50kg (110lb) SC 50 bombs carried on racks underneath the wings. Using an adaptor, the centreline station could also accommodate four SC 50s.

Typical tactics employed on the Eastern Front included running in to the target at around 483km/h (300mph) at a height of around 9m (30ft) above the ground, before releasing a bomb as the vehicle disappeared from view beneath the engine cowling. In this way, an SC 250 weapon would likely either score a direct hit on a tank or would ricochet off the ground before hitting the vehicle. Using a one-second delay on the fuse permitted the Fw 190F time to pull up and provide clearance from the blast and fragments. Once the bomb(s) had been released, the Fw 190F pilot would often remain on the scene, using the cannon and machine guns to destroy any soft-skin vehicles that might be supporting the armour and troops in the area. In most cases, it was the soft-skin vehicles that were the pilot's primary targets, since removing these would hopefully deprive the tanks of their fuel and ammunition.

The initial Fw 190F-1 was a development of the Fw 190A-4, while the Fw 190F-2 was based on the Fw 190A-5 and fitted with a bulged canopy for improved visibility. The Fw 190F-3 was developed from the Fw 190A-6 and could carry a 250kg (551lb) bomb or drop tank below the fuselage, supplemented by four ETC 50 underwing bomb racks

A *Staffel* of Fw 190Fs at Deplin-Irena Airfield near Warsaw. Ground attack units rotated through the airfield to conduct training missions using live ordnance at the nearby bombing range prior to frontline deployment.

(Fw 190F-3/R1) or a pair of underwing 30mm (1.18in) MK 103 cannon (Fw 190F-3/R3).

Ground-attack variant

Around 550 Fw 190F-1, F-2 and F-3 aircraft were built between late 1942 and mid-1943, before production switched to the Fw 190G. However, a growing demand for ground-attack aircraft meant the Fw 190F-8 returned to production in spring 1944. Based on the Fw 190A-8, the F-8 had two fuselage-mounted MG 131 machine guns and four ETC 50 bomb racks. There was also a pair of anti-shipping

variants: the Fw 190F-8/U2 and U3 with provision for torpedo carriage, respectively armed with the 700kg (1543lb) BT 700 or the 1400kg (3086lb) BT 1400 weapons.

Last of the line was the Fw 190F-9, introduced in mid-1944 – otherwise similar to the F-8, it was powered by a BMW 801TS/TH engine.

In April 1945 as the war in Europe drew to a close, the Luftwaffe could call upon 1612 Fw 190s – although shortages of manpower and fuel remained critical. Of these aircraft, 809 were Fw 190F and Fw 190G ground-attack variants.

Focke-Wulf Fw 190F-8

This Fw 190F-8 of 6./Schlachtgeschwader 2 was flown by *Hauptmann* Günther Bleckmann.

Focke-Wulf 190F-8

Weight (Maximum take-off) 4900kg (10,800lb)

Dimensions Length: 8.95m (29ft 3in), Wingspan: 10.49m (34ft 5in), Height: 3.96m (13ft)

Powerplant One 1268kW (1700hp) BMW 801D-2 18-cylinder two row radial

Speed 653km/h (408mph)

Range 900km (560 miles)

Ceiling 11,410m (37,400ft)

Crew 1

Armament Two 13mm (0.51in) MG 131 machine guns, two 20mm (0.8in) MG 151/20 cannon; ETC 501 bomb rack as centerline mount and four ETC 50 bomb racks as underwing mounts

---

A close-up view of the Fw 190's fuselage bomb rack loaded with an SC 250 general purpose bomb.

Focke-Wulf Fw 190F-2

Operating over Kharkov on the Eastern Front in 1943, this Fw 190F-2 was among the dedicated close-support versions that replaced the Ju 87 in this role. This particular aircraft was operated by the 5. Staffel, II. Gruppe of Schlachtgeschwader 1.

Powerplant
Based on the Fw 190A-5 airframe, the Fw 190F-2 was powered by the BMW 801D-2 14-cylinder two-row radial engine accommodated in a lengthened mounting.

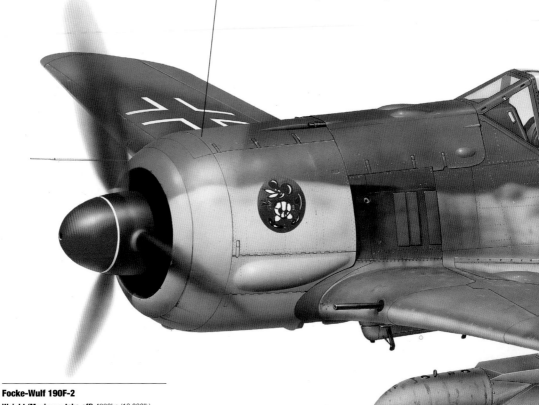

Focke-Wulf 190F-2

Weight (Maximum take-off) 4900kg (10,800lb)

Dimensions Length: 8.84m (29ft), Wingspan: 10.49m (34ft 5in), Height: 3.96m (13ft)

Powerplant One 1268kW (1700hp) BMW 801D-2 18-cylinder two row radial

Speed 653km/h (408mph)

Range 900km (560 miles)

Ceiling 11,410m (37,400ft)

Crew 1

Armament Four 20mm (0.8in) MG 151/20 cannon; two 7.92mm (0.3in) MGs; two 1800kg (3968lb) bombs

Bomb
The early Fw 190F carried a single bomb on an ETC 501 fuselage rack or four smaller disposable stores on an ER 4 adaptor.

Tailfin
The robust fin was comprised of two spars, one vertical along the rear and one angled along the leading edge. The rudder ran the full length of the fin.

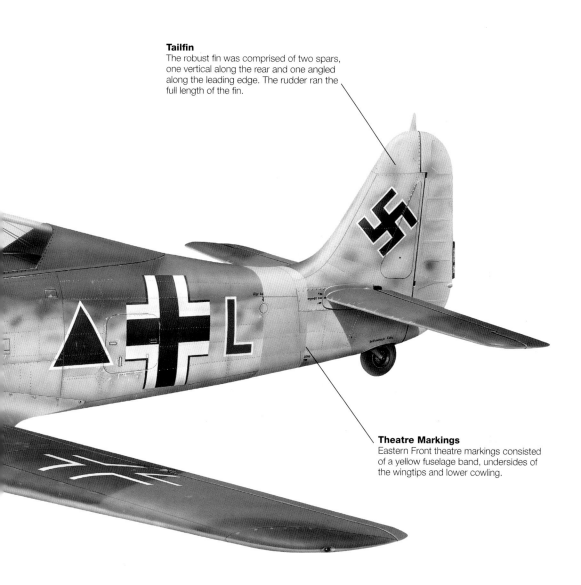

Theatre Markings
Eastern Front theatre markings consisted of a yellow fuselage band, undersides of the wingtips and lower cowling.

Focke-Wulf Fw 190G

Developed in parallel with the Fw 190F that was destined for the *Schlachtgeschwader*, the Fw 190G was an extended-range fighter-bomber version with provision for a drop tank beneath each wing.

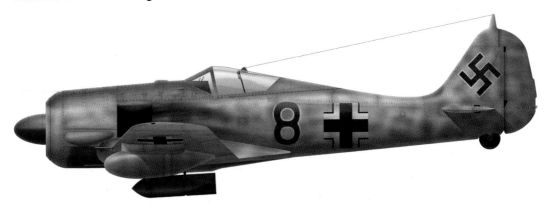

In Luftwaffe parlance, the new version was designated as a *Jagdbomber mit vergrösserter Reichweite* (abbreviated to *Jabo-Rei*) – or fighter-bomber with extended range. Prior to being approved for production, the Fw 190G underwent trials against a modified Bf 109G – the Fieseler/Skoda FiSk

199, or Bf 109G-2/R1, which added external fuel tanks and an additional undercarriage leg to provide clearance for larger bombloads. The Focke-Wulf design proved itself to be far superior for the *Jabo-Rei* role.

The additional weight of the external fuel led to the deletion of

This Fw 190G-1 is equipped with 300-litre (66-Imp gal) fuel tanks and a 250kg (551lb) bomb. It was probably operated by II./Schlachtgeschwader 4, based at Viterbo, Italy, in November 1943.

Focke-Wulf 190G-1

Weight (Maximum take-off) 4900kg (10,800lb)

Dimensions Length: 8.84m (29ft), Wingspan: 10.50m (34ft 5in), Height: 3.96m (13ft)

Powerplant One 1267kW (1700hp) BMW 801D-2 piston engine

Speed 654km/h (408mph)

Range 800km (500 miles)

Ceiling 10,600m (34,776ft)

Crew 1

Armament Two 20mm (0.8in) MG 151/20 cannon; either one 250kg (550lb) or one 500kg (1102lb) bomb on the centreline and one 250kg (550lb) bomb under each wing

---

This Fw 190G-3 carries a single 500kg (1102lb) SC500 bomb and a pair of 300 litre (66 gallon) fuel tanks. Fixed armament was reduced to just two MG 151/20 cannons.

machine guns from the fuselage of the Fw 190G, leaving it with a reduced basic armament of just two 20mm (0.8in) MG 151 cannon in the wing roots. The G-series also retained the armour protection introduced on the Fw 190F. Most of the Fw 190Gs were equipped with a power boosting system, with either the MW50 water-methanol injection system for low-level operations or the bulkier GM-1 kit for nitrous-oxide boost at high altitude.

Fw 190G-1

The Fw 190G-1 was a fighter-bomber derivative of the Fw 190A-5. It could carry 1800kg (3968lb) of bombs, which required strengthened landing gear. Wing-mounted armament was reduced to two MG 151/20 cannon, while Junkers-designed underwing racks could accommodate a pair of 300-litre (66-Imp gal) drop tanks.

While the majority of Fw 190Gs would serve on the Eastern Front, the version first saw combat in North Africa, to where it was rushed following the Allied Torch landings of November 1942. The initial unit to fly the G-series in this theatre was Schlachtgeschwader 2 'Immelmann',

based at Zarzoun in Tunisia. Once deployed in numbers in the east, Fw 190Gs served during the huge armoured battles around Kursk in July 1943. By October the same year, the *Schlachtgeschwader* had undergone a restructuring under the command of *Oberst* Hubertus Hitschold. From now on, all Ju 87s – apart from the anti-armour-optimized Ju 87G – would be removed from frontline duties, to be replaced by the Fw 190F and G.

Otherwise similar to the Fw 190G-1, the G-2 utilized Messerschmitt-designed racks for the underwing drop tanks. In late summer 1943 the next in the G-series arrived: this made use of Focke-Wulf drop tank racks and was fitted with autopilot and a balloon cable cutter.

Last in the series

The last of the G-series to see quantity production was the Fw 190G-8 which, as its designation suggests, was

based on the Fw 190A-8 and was powered by the 1342kW (1800hp) BMW 801D-2 engine.

By May 1944 there were a total of 881 Fw 190s assigned to Luftwaffe units. Of these, 387, or almost half, were Fw 190F and G models operated by ground-attack and fighter-bomber units. By early the following year, most Fw 190G-1s, G-3s and G-8s were regularly carrying 1000kg (2204lb) bombs, while the 1800kg (3968lb) SC 1800 weapon was first used on 7 March 1945 during attacks on the bridge over the Rhine at Remagen.

Focke-Wulf 190G-3

Weight (Maximum take-off) 4900kg (10,800lb)
Dimensions Length: 8.84m (29ft), Wingspan: 10.50m (34ft 5in), Height: 3.96m (13ft)
Powerplant One 1267kW (1700hp) BMW 801D-2 piston engine
Speed 654km/h (408mph)
Range 800km (500 miles)
Ceiling 10,600m (34,776ft)
Crew 1
Armament Two 20mm (0.8in) MG 151/20 cannon; either one 250kg (550lb) or one 500kg (1,100lb) bomb on the centreline and one 250kg (550lb) bomb under each wing

---

Focke-Wulf Fw 190G-3

Fw 190G-3 DN+FP (*Werknummer* 160043) was operated by III./Schnellkampfgeschwader 10 based at Montecorvino Rovella, Italy, in September 1943.

Focke-Wulf Ta 152

Reflecting Kurt Tank's overall design responsibility for the Fw 190 family, and a change in fighter aircraft designations ordered by the *Reichsluftfahrtministerium* (German Air Ministry), the Ta 152 name was introduced for the ultimate 'long-nose' development of the series.

This was derived from the abortive Fw 190C and the abandoned Ta 153 proposal, the latter emerging as a single development prototype powered by a DB 603 engine and with an all-new high-aspect-ratio wing of increased span. Other changes in the Ta 153 included a revised structure for the fuselage and tail and improved internal systems. In the event, it was judged that production of the Ta 153 would have an adverse effect of existing Fw 190 production and instead focus was placed on the Ta 152. This was developed from the Fw 190D, with the aim of further improving performance at high altitude through a series of airframe refinements, but with the basic structure inherited from the 'Dora', except for the flap and undercarriage systems which featured hydraulic, rather than electrical actuation. The Ta 152 retained the hub-firing 30mm (1.18in) cannon of the 'Dora' but introduced improved electrical systems and other refinements.

As originally planned, there was to be a high-altitude Ta 152H powered by a Jumo 213E-1 and a Ta 152B with the Jumo 213C for work at lower levels.

Prototypes of the Ta 152H (H for *Höhenjäger*, or 'high-altitude fighter') entered flight testing in late June 1944 with the long-span wing of high aspect ratio.

The first of the pre-production batch of 20 Ta 152H-0s was completed at Focke-Wulf's Cottbus factory and took to the air in October 1944. Service trials of these long-span aircraft were undertaken by Eprobungskommando 152 at Rechlin. The last of the Ta 152H-0s was apparently used to test a new revolver cannon, the MG 213, which would form the basis of the post-war Aden and DEFA guns.

Jet fighter escort

The Ta 152H-1 was armed with a single 30mm (1.18in) and two 20mm (0.8in) cannon and could achieve a top speed of 760km/h (472mph) at a height of 12,500m (41,010ft). This exceptional performance was aided by the type's extended wingspan.

However, only around a dozen examples of the Ta 152H-1 were completed and were delivered to JG 301 by the time the war in Europe came to an end. This unit was tasked

Focke-Wulf Ta 152H-1

The 'H' variant of the Focke-Wulf Ta 152 was a high-altitude fighter. Small numbers were operated by Jagdgeschwader 301, primarily to provide cover over Messerschmitt Me 262 bases while the jets were taking off and landing.

Focke-Wulf Ta 152H-1

Weight (Maximum take-off) 4727kg (10,421lb)
Dimensions Length: 10.82m (35ft 6in), Wingspan: 14.44m (47ft 5in), Height: 3.36m (11ft)
Powerplant One 1530kW (2050hp) Junkers Jumo 213E-1 liquid-cooled piston engine
Speed 760km/h (472mph)
Range 2000km (1200 miles)
Ceiling 15,100m (49,500ft) with GM-1 boost
Crew 1
Armament One 30mm (1.18in) MK 108 cannon, two 20mm (0.8in) MG 151/20 cannon

with the protection of bases used by the Messerschmitt Me 262 jet fighter, which required close escort during the vulnerable take-off and landing phases. This was clearly a wasteful use of a fighter that offered superb high-altitude capabilities, while other examples were directed to ground-attack duties. In one dramatic episode that demonstrated the performance of the Ta 152H, Kurt Tank himself was flying an example on a test flight when he was 'bounced' by a flight of P-51D Mustangs. The designer was able to escape effortlessly, simply opening the throttle and waiting for the American fighters to become 'no more than two dots on the horizon'.

C-series

While the lower-level Ta 152B was abandoned, the concept re-emerged as the Ta 153C-0, a short-span fighter with the Jumo 213C replaced by a 1720kW (2300hp) DB 603 engine. The extra length of the engine was compensated for by a rear-fuselage plug and enlarged tail surfaces, as in the Fw 190D-9.

Production versions with standard wing comprised the Ta 153C-1, the C-2 with improved radio equipment and the C-3 with revised armament, the previous 30mm (1.18in) engine-mounted MK 108 being replaced by an MK 103 cannon. The C-series aircraft were also fitted with four 20mm (0.8in) MG 151/20 guns, two above the engine and two in the wing roots, while the H-series carried only two 20mm (0.8in) cannon, plus the hub-firing weapon. The additional weapons on the Ta 152C resulted in inferior speed and turn rate, but provided enough firepower to cope with most of the bomber targets it was expected to encounter. A point of differentiation between the Ta 152C-1 and the H-1

was the position of the air inlet: that of the C-1's DB 603 was located on the left, while that of the H-1's Jumo was positioned on the right.

Other derivatives of the basic Ta 152 included the Ta 152S-1, a two-seat conversion trainer, and the Ta 152E that was planned as a reconnaissance fighter version of the Ta 152C, again with the standard wing. The Ta 152E-2 was a high-altitude fighter with the H-series wing and a Jumo 213E powerplant.

Total production of the Ta 152 amounted to a reported 26 prototypes together with 67 production and pre-production aircraft.

Long-span wings gave the final variant of the Focke-Wulf Fw 190/Ta 152 family, the Ta 152H, a superb high-altitude performance.

Dewoitine D.520

The French-designed D.520 fell into German hands once the Vichy air arm was demobilized on 27 November 1942 following the Allied landings in North Africa and the Nazis' seizure of unoccupied France.

A total of 1876 French aircraft were sequestrated by the Germans, among them 246 D.520 single-engine fighters. At the same time, manufacturer SNCASE were ordered to continue work on 150 examples that were still under construction.

German service

The D.520 saw extensive use with the Axis air forces and although the Luftwaffe initially put it to use as a fighter trainer, it also saw some combat with the *Jagdgeschwader* (fighter wings) on the Eastern Front. Other D.520s were redirected by Germany to the air arms of Bulgaria, Italy and Romania.

The D.520 was a cantilever low-wing monoplane that was a much-improved development of the previous D.513 fighter, characterized by a much cleaner engine installation and a new wing with increased dihedral and straight-tapered leading and training edges. It showed great potential and, once the first of three prototype D.520s took to the air on 2 October 1938, an order was quickly placed for 200 D.520C.1 fighters, later increased to 710. These aircraft were to be powered by a 967kW (935hp) Hispano-Suiza 12Y-45 engine with supercharger, and the first example flew in October 1939.

The D.520 was the most capable and modern fighter available to France at the time of the outbreak of the war but only 300 examples had been delivered by mid-June 1940. By the time of the armistice with Germany on 25 June 1940, 403 aircraft were on strength.

Dewoitine D.520

This D.520 flew with Jagdgeschwader 101, a Jagdfliegerschule unit based at Pau-Nord, Pyrénées-Atlantiques, France, March 1944.

Dewoitine D.520C.1
Weight (Maximum take-off) 2677kg (5902lb)
Dimensions Length: 8.6m (28ft 3in), Wingspan: 10.2m (33ft 6in), Height: 2.57m (8ft 5in)
Powerplant One 967kW (935hp) Hispano-Suiza 12Y-45 engine with supercharger
Speed 560 km/h (350 mph)
Range 1250km (780 miles)
Ceiling 10,000m (33,000ft)
Crew 1
Armament One 20mm (0.8in) Hispano-Suiza HS.404 cannon, plus four 7.5mm (0.29in) MAC 1934 machine guns

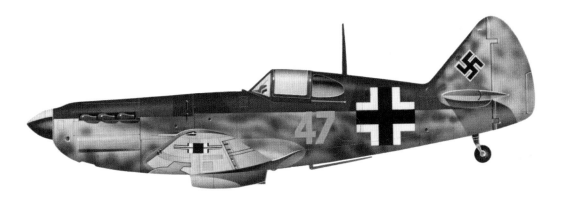

Dewoitine D.520

A D.520 of Jagdgeschwader 105, based in Chartres,
Eure-et-Loir, France, May 1944.

Dornier Do 335 *Pfeil*

A tandem-engine layout had been patented by Claudius Dornier in 1937 and led to feasibility trials with the Göppingen Gö 9 research aircraft designed by Ulrich Hütter and built by Schempp-Hirth in 1939.

Impressed with the potential of the pusher-puller configuration, the German Air Ministry selected the layout for its Dornier Do P.231 bomber project.

Work on the P.231 was cancelled at a relatively advanced stage and attention now turned to a tandem-engine fighter, as Dornier had originally envisaged. The high-performance fighter was a low-wing cantilever monoplane of all-metal construction with a cruciform tail unit and tricycle landing gear. Power was provided by two 1342kW (1800hp) Daimler-Benz DB 603 engines, one in the rear fuselage driving a three-bladed pusher propeller and the other in the nose with a three-bladed tractor propeller.

The first prototype Do 335 *Pfeil* ('arrow'), Do 335 V1, took to the air in October 1943 before embarking on

trials at Rechlin and Oberpfaffenhofen. The fifth prototype, Do 335 V5, was the first to feature armament: a pair of 20mm (0.8in) MG 151 cannon in the upper fuselage decking and a single 30mm (1.18in) MK 103 cannon firing through the forward propeller hub.

Pre-production batch

After nine prototypes, work began on a pre-production batch of 10 Do 335A-0 aircraft, the first of which was ready for evaluation in mid-1944.

Production of the Do 335 encompassed a range of different versions, none of which were built in quantity. The full-production Do 335A-1 first appeared in late autumn 1944, with the definitive DB 603E-1 engine and two underwing hardpoints able to carry either drop tanks or 250kg (551lb) bombs. A single example of the

unarmed Do 335A-4 reconnaissance version was also completed, with provision for additional internal fuel and two cameras in an under-fuselage bay. The Do 335A-6 was next to appear, as the first of a night fighter version. This had FuG 217J Neptun airborne intercept radar installed with aerials forward of the wing and a second crewman added in a cockpit above and behind the pilot.

Final variants

The last of the Do 335 variants to be completed were the Do 335A-10 and A-12, both of which featured the second cockpit that was introduced on the Do 335A-6 night fighter, but which were intended for training rather than combat use. While the Do 335A-10 was powered by DB 603A engines, the A12 employed the DB 603E. Both were fitted with dual controls and while the prototypes were unarmed, a pair of Do 335A-12 production aircraft had the cannon reinstated.

The closest the *Pfeil* came to combat service was when it was issued to the operational test unit, Eprobungskommando 335, in spring 1945. Under study were a number of advanced developments of the basic design to fulfil two-seat night fighter (Do 345) and long-range reconnaissance (Do 635) roles, the latter making use of two Do 335

airframes mated together via a new wing centre-section.

Meanwhile, the Do 335 was envisaged as a mixed-power fighter to be developed in conjunction with Heinkel, the rear piston engine being replaced by a turbojet.

Dornier Do 335V1 Pfeil

The Do 335 V1 first prototype, bearing the *Stammkennzeichen* (factory radio code) of CP+UA, was flown on 26 October 1943 by test pilot *Flugkapitän* Hans Dieterle.

Dornier Do 335A-0

Weight (Maximum take-off) 9600kg (21,164lb)
Dimensions Length: 13.85m (45ft 5in), Wingspan: 13.8m (45ft 3in), Height: 5m (16ft 5in)
Powerplant Two 1417kW (1900hp) Daimler-Benz DB 603E-1 V-12 liquid-cooled piston engines
Speed 763km/h (474mph)
Range 1395km (867 miles)
Ceiling 11,400m (37,400ft)
Crew 1
Armament One engine-mounted 30mm (1.18in) MK 103 cannon plus two 20mm (0.79in) MG 151/20 cannon; up to 1000kg (2200lb) bombload in internal weapons bay

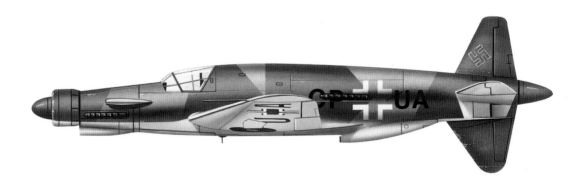

Dornier Do 335A-0

Below is the seventh of 10 pre-production aircraft, most of which went to Eprobungskommando (EK) 335 for evaluation.

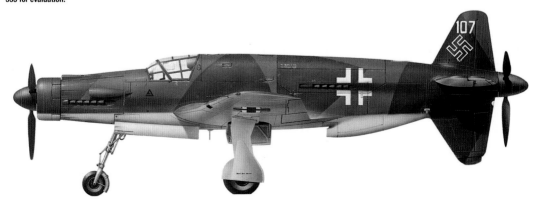

Blohm und Voss BV 40

Designed by Richard Vogt, the BV 40 was one of several designs submitted to the *Reichsluftfahrtministerium* (German Air Ministry) in 1943.

It was developed as a single-seat glider fighter as the German war machine sought to conserve its dwindling resources of strategic materials. The design of the BV 40 was also intended for survivability, allowing head-on attacks to be made against the Allied bomber streams that were having a devastating effect on German infrastructure. As a result, the aircraft had the minimum possible frontal area – the engine was deleted entirely, and the aircraft was flown by a prone pilot. Early tests showed that, despite being unpowered, the BV 40 would be able to achieve a speed of 900km/h (560mph) in a dive.

The aircraft featured a heavily armoured cockpit, metal centre fuselage and wooden rear fuselage, wings and tail surfaces. Twin-wheel landing gear was provided but was

Blohm und Voss BV 40V-1

The first prototype BV 40 V1, PN+UA, as it appeared at the Blohm & Voss plant in March 1944.

jettisoned at take-off, the glider returning to its airfield on a semi-retractable skid.

Towed fighter

In practice, it was hoped that the small frontal area of the BV 40 would allow the pilot to press home an attack on a bomber unnoticed, before opening fire with the two 30mm (1.18in) MK 108 cannon mounted in the wing roots. The fighter would reach its target after being towed to altitude – singly or in pairs – by a Messerschmitt Bf 109G fighter. Once above and ahead of the bomber formation, the glider would attack head-on in a 20 degree dive. Another option called for one of the guns to be removed and replaced by an explosive charge, carried on a cable, which would detonate after snagging a bomber.

Although 19 prototypes and 200 production aircraft were ordered, only six test specimens joined the trials programme. The initial example, BV

40 V1, completed a first flight (towed aloft by a Bf 110) in May 1944. The test programme was almost complete when the entire project was cancelled in autumn 1944.

Blohm und Voss BV 40V-1

Weight (Maximum take-off) 952kg (2099lb)
Dimensions Length: 5.7m (18ft 8in), Wingspan: 7.9m (25ft 11in), Height: 1.63m (5ft 4in)
Powerplant N/A
Speed 900km/h (560mph)
Range N/A
Ceiling N/A
Crew 1
Armament Two 30mm (1.18in) MK 108 cannon

HEAVY FIGHTERS

The Luftwaffe entered the heavy fighter category with the Messerschmitt Bf 110 *Zerstörer* (destroyer) in the mid-1930s. Although the concept was found wanting when faced with single-seat fighter opposition, the German air arm never gave up on its twin-engine fighters, fielding them in numerous roles. By the end of the war, the German aero industry had produced a range of highly efficient night-fighter adaptations of the Bf 110 and Junkers Ju 88 in particular.

This chapter includes the following aircraft:
- Messerschmitt Bf 110
- Focke-Wulf Fw 187 *Falke*
- Dornier Do 17
- Dornier Do 215
- Dornier Do 217
- Junkers Ju 88
- Focke-Wulf Ta 154
- Heinkel He 219 *Uhu*
- Arado Ar 240
- Messerschmitt Me 210
- Messerschmitt Me 410

Messerschmitt Bf 110 D-3s from Zerstörergeschwader 76 (ZG 76) painted with shark nose art stand at an airfield in Greece, 1941.

Messerschmitt Bf 110 early production

With the Luftwaffe seeking a new twin-engine fighter, the Bayerische Flugzeugwerke (later Messerschmitt) responded in summer 1935 with its Bf 110 design, which would compete with rival submissions from Focke-Wulf and Henschel.

The new warplane was primarily intended for use as a heavy fighter, but it was expected to have the versatility to serve as a high-speed bomber in a secondary role when required. As the requirement was fine-tuned, both the Focke-Wulf and Henschel entrants fell by the wayside, and it was left to Messerschmitt to produce three prototypes of its all-metal, twin-engine candidate. A maiden flight by the initial prototype, the Bf 110 V1, was recorded on 12 May 1936, with Rudolf Opitz at the controls. Although the original pair of 679kW (910hp) Daimler-Benz DB 600A engines proved very unreliable, the basic aircraft showed great promise, including demonstrating a speed of 505km/h (314mph) at an altitude of 3175m (10,415ft) in early tests, outperforming the single-seat Bf 109B-2 fighter.

The second prototype, the Bf 110 V2, featured some refinements and was sent to Rechlin for service evaluation in January 1937. The third and final prototype, the Bf 110 V3, served as an armament testbed with four 7.92mm (0.31in) MG 17 machine guns in the nose; it completed its maiden flight in December 1936.

Pre-series Bf 110A-0

Despite continuing powerplant reliability problems afflicting the first three prototypes, these aircraft were followed by the pre-series Bf 110A-0, now powered by Junkers Jumo 210Da engines, each of which developed 507kW (680hp). While these engines were more reliable that the DB 600A units, their reduced output imposed a considerable performance penalty. The programme would be subject to severe delays before the much-improved fuel-injection DB 601A engine became available, and the Bf 110B series retained the Jumo powerplant.

Following completion of the last of the four pre-production Bf 110A-0 machines in March 1938, focus

switched to the B-model. This featured a range of aerodynamic improvements and introduced a pair of 20mm (0.8in) cannon to supplement the four machine guns of the Bf 110A-0. An initial pre-production Bf 110B-0 took to the air on 19 April 1938, powered by a pair of Jumo 210Ga engines.

Bf 110B model

The first of the series-production B-model variants was the Bf 110B-

---

Messerschmitt Bf 110B-1

Weight (Maximum take-off) 6749kg (14,880lb)

Dimensions Length: 12m (39ft 7in), Wingspan: 16.2m (53ft 2in), Height: 4m (13ft 6in)

Powerplant Two 515kW (690hp) Junkers Jumo 210Ga engines

Speed 475km/h (295mph)

Range 774km (481 miles)

Ceiling 10,000m (32,810ft)

Crew 2

Armament Two 20mm (0.8in) Oerlikon MG FF cannon, four 7.92mm (0.31in) MG 17 machine guns, one 7.92mm (0.31in) MG 15 (rear of cockpit)

This Messerschmitt Bf 110-0 shows the type's slim fuselage and graceful lines.

1, which retained the Jumo 210Ga engines and began to come off the Augsburg production line in summer 1938. Basic armament comprised a pair of 20mm (0.8in) Oerlikon MG FF cannon and four MG 17 machine guns; the rear gunner was additionally provided with a single 7.92mm (0.31in) MG 15 firing from the rear cockpit. The Bf 110B-1 was the first of the line

to enter active service, being issued to *schweren Jagdgruppen* – the Luftwaffe's heavy fighter groups – as of autumn 1938.

The Bf 110B-1 was followed by the Bf 110B-2 with a camera in place of the 20mm (0.8in) cannon for the reconnaissance role. A number of Bf 110B-1 aircraft were further modified to serve as two-seat

Messerschmitt Bf 110B-1

This Bf 110B-1 was operated by the one of the *Zerstörerschulen* (*Zerstörer* schools), based at Nancy, France, in 1940.

crew trainers under the Bf 110B-3 designation; these had their armament removed and improved radio and instruments added.

Messerschmitt Bf 110C/D

The availability of the 820kW (1100hp) Daimler-Benz DB 601A engine with fuel injection provided the impetus to produce the Bf 110C series.

This started out in the form of 10 pre-production Bf 110C-0 aircraft that were delivered for evaluation in January 1939, with DB 601A-1 engines. Soon after, they were followed by a series-production batch of Bf 110C-1 fighters, with the same powerplant combined with the two-cannon, four-machine gun primary armament of the Bf 110B-1. As the production effort ramped up, Focke-Wulf and Gotha both joined the programme.

The first Bf 110C-0 pre-production aircraft were delivered to the newly created *Zerstörergruppen* (heavy fighter groups, formerly *schweren Jagdgruppen*) in early 1939. By the outbreak of World War II, the Bf 110C-1 was in service with I./

(Zerst)/Lehrgeschwader Nr 1, I./ Zerstörergeschwader Nr 1 and I./ZG 76, with each group having two squadrons of Bf 110C-1s and another conversion unit with Bf 110B-3 trainers.

C-series combat debut

The C-series saw its combat debut during the invasion of Poland in September 1939 and cemented its early reputation when examples shot down no fewer than 22 Royal Air Force Wellington bombers on a mission over the Heligoland Bight in December the same year.

The Luftwaffe assigned a high priority to the heavy fighter and a total of 315 aircraft had been delivered by the end of 1939. Throughout the

following year, production averaged 102 aircraft per month.

Subvariants of the C-series included the Bf 110C-1 to C-7, of which the Bf 110C-2 featured improved radio and the Bf 110C-3 introduced improved Oerlikon MG FF/M cannon. The Bf 110C-4 provided the pilot with additional armour plating, its Bf 110C-4/B subvariant being intended to serve as a fighter-bomber, with two ETC 250 racks under the fuselage and powerplant of two DB 601N-1 engines each rated at 895kW (1200hp).

The Bf 110C-5 was a reconnaissance aircraft with a single camera and reduced armament, while the Bf 110C-5/N was similar but with the DB 601N-1 powerplant. The Bf

110C-6 had the twin 20mm (0.8in) cannon replaced by a single 30mm (1.18in) MK 101 cannon; the last of the C-models, the Bf 110C-7, was essentially similar to the Bf 110C-4/B but with strengthened landing gear and two ETC 500 belly racks for a larger bombload.

The subsequent Bf 110D series was intended for long-range operations

Messerschmitt Bf 110C-7

Weight (Maximum take-off) 6749kg (14,880lb)

Dimensions Length: 13.05m (42ft 9in), Wingspan: 16.25m (53ft 4in), Height: 4.18m (13ft 8in)

Powerplant Two 895kW (1200hp) Daimler-Benz DB 601N-1 12-cylinder inverted-V type engine

Speed 550km/h (342mph)

Range 1300km (808 miles)

Ceiling 8000m (26,245ft)

Crew 2

Armament Two 20mm (0.8in) MG FF/M cannon, four 7.92mm (0.31in) MG 17 machine guns, one 7.92mm (0.31in) MG 15 machine gun; two ETC 500 centreline bomb racks capable of carrying two 250, 500, or 1000kg (2,204lb) bombs

and included the pre-series Bf 110D-0. Of the series-production aircraft that followed, the Bf 110D-1/R1 subvariant was outfitted with a 1200-litre (264 Imp gal) external belly tank for extended-range missions; the Bf 110D-1/R2 was equipped to carry a pair of 900-litre (198 Imp gal) underwing drop tanks; the Bf 110D-2 was a long-range fighter-bomber with ETC 500 racks and provision for two 300-litre (66 Imp gal) drop tanks; while the Bf 110D-3 was envisaged for the convoy escort role, with either two 300-litre or two 900-litre tanks and provision for a life-raft in the tail cone.

However, 1940 also saw the tables turned on the Bf 110 – and the Luftwaffe heavy fighter concept – for

Messerschmitt Bf 110C-1

Weight (Maximum take-off) 6749kg (14,880lb)

Dimensions Length: 12m (39ft 7in), Wingspan: 16.2m (53ft 2in), Height: 4.13m (13ft 7in)

Powerplant Two 780kW (1050hp) DB 601A-1 V-12 liquid-cooled piston engines

Speed 475km/h (295mph)

Range 774km (481 miles)

Ceiling 10,000m (32,810ft)

Crew 2

Armament Two 20mm (0.8in) MG FF/M cannon, four 7.92mm (0.31in) MG 17 machine guns, one 7.92mm (0.31in) MG 15 machine gun

the first time. Once it encountered modern single-engine fighters like the RAF's Hurricane and Spitfire en masse, the Bf 110 was quickly found wanting. It lacked the manoeuvrability of the single-engine fighters and with only a single rearward-firing machine

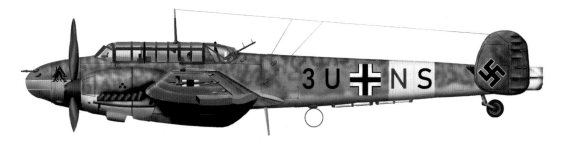

gun for defence it was also hopelessly outgunned. From the start of the Battle of Britain in summer 1940, Luftwaffe Bf 110 losses began to mount. As that campaign continued, the type was increasingly switched to bombing and reconnaissance missions, but by the winter of 1940–41 it had found a new niche as a night fighter.

Early night fighters

The first of the Bf 110 night fighters were unchanged from the basic heavy fighter versions and were simply flown at night as a counter to the growing threat of Allied night bombing raids. By mid-1941, the Bf 110 night fighter was beginning to operate under the guidance of a ground-controlled interception network. Around 12 months later, the night fighter units began to be issued with Lichtenstein air

interception radar and most Luftwaffe fighters in this role were carrying a version of this radar by autumn 1942. The RAF's response to Luftwaffe night fighter radar was the radar-jamming Window – consisting of bundles of aluminium foil strips. This proved effective for around six months, until the Luftwaffe's Bf 110s began using more capable radar.

By early 1944, the Luftwaffe's night fighter arm was at its zenith, and around 320 Bf 110s were deployed in the nocturnal defence of Germany, equivalent to around 60 per cent of total night fighter strength.

In the final year of the war, the introduction of more advanced night fighters had relegated the Bf 110's importance, to the extent that only 150 examples remained operational with the night-fighter groups.

Messerschmitt Bf 110D-3

Operating in support of the *Deutsches Afrika Korps*, this Bf 110D-3 was assigned to 8./ Zerstörergeschwader 26 during 1941.

Messerschmitt Bf 110D-3

Weight (Maximum take-off) 6749kg (14,880lb)
Dimensions Length: 13.05m (42ft 9in), Wingspan: 16.25m (53ft 4in), Height: 4.18m (13ft 8in)
Powerplant Two 895kW (1200hp) Daimler-Benz DB 601N 12 cylinder inverted-V type engine
Speed 550km/h (342mph)
Range 1300km (808 miles)
Ceiling 8000m (26,245ft)
Crew 2
Armament Two 20mm (0.79in) cannon, four 7.92mm (0.31in) MGs in nose, one 7.92mm (0.31in) MG in rear cockpit; provision for two 900 litre (198 Imp gal) fuel tanks

---

Messerschmitt Bf 110C-1 aircraft from 2./ZG 26 fly over Wilno in northeast Poland during Operation 'Barbarossa', July 1941.

Messerschmitt Bf 110C-4/B

This aircraft flew with II Gruppe, Erprobungsgruppe
210, deployed in raids across the English
Channel in the summer of 1940. It features the
famous *Wespen* ('wasp') nose markings of
Zerstörergeschwader 1.

Cockpit
The cockpit of the Bf 110 was designed for a crew
of three, comprising, from front to rear, a pilot, radio
operator and rear gunner.

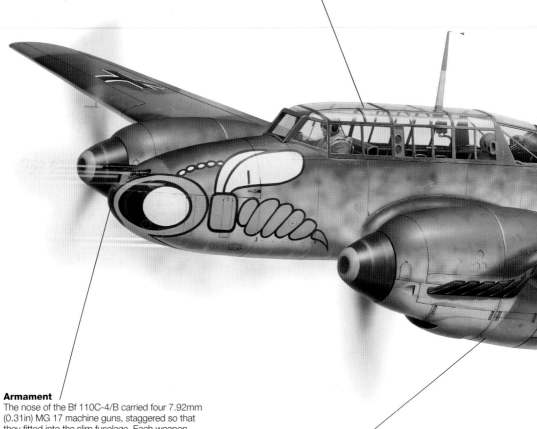

Armament
The nose of the Bf 110C-4/B carried four 7.92mm
(0.31in) MG 17 machine guns, staggered so that
they fitted into the slim fuselage. Each weapon
had 1000 rounds of ammunitions, held in
magazines beneath the guns.

Engine
Early models of the Bf 110 featured a deep
radiator bath under each engine, but the Bf 110C
introduced shallow glycol radiators under the
wings, outboard of each engine.

Messerschmitt Bf 110C-4/B

Weight (Maximum take-off) 6749kg (14,880lb)

Dimensions Length: 13.05m (42ft 9in), Wingspan: 16.25m (53ft 4in), Height: 4.18m (13ft 8in)

Powerplant Two 895kW (1200hp) Daimler-Benz DB 601N 12 cylinder inverted-V type engine

Speed 550km/h (342mph)

Range 1300km (808 miles)

Ceiling 8000m (26,245ft)

Crew 2

Armament Two 20mm (0.8in) cannon, four 7.92mm (0.31in) MGs in nose, one 7.92mm (0.31in) MG in rear cockpit; two 250kg (550lb) bombs

Tail Wing
The Bf 110's tail was mounted simply on top of the rear fuselage.

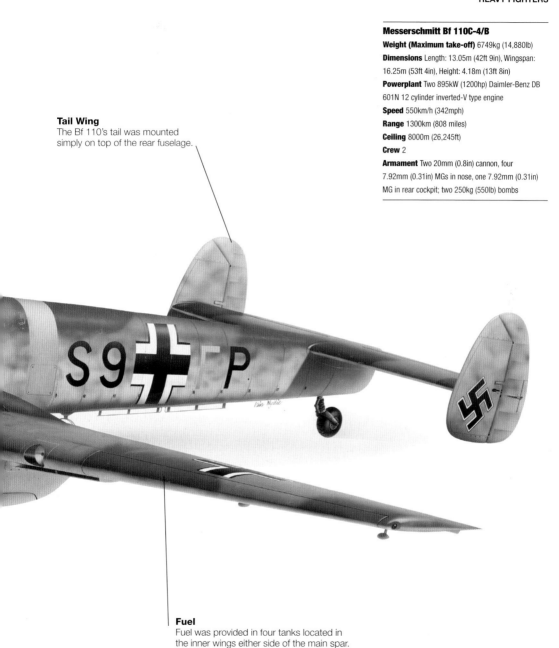

Fuel
Fuel was provided in four tanks located in the inner wings either side of the main spar. The forward tanks each held 373 litres (82 gallons), while the rear tanks each held 264 litres (58 Imp gallons).

Messerschmitt Bf 110E/F

The Bf 110E production series arrived when production of the aircraft's intended successor, the Me 210A-1, was already under way. The Bf 110E, and the Bf 110F series that followed, both featured bolstered armament and increased power.

They continued to serve – albeit in dwindling numbers – during the campaigns in North Africa and on the Eastern Front.

The E-series included subvariants comprising the Bf 110E-1 night fighter and Bf 110E-2 fighter-bomber and the Bf 110E-3 long-range reconnaissance aircraft. When it entered service, the Bf 110E-1 was the definitive fighter-bomber version, with an additional four ETC 50 bomb racks under the wings and a bombload increased to 1200kg (2645lb). Power was initially provided by two DB 601A-1s, later superseded by a pair of DB 601N-1 engines. Other changes addressed ancillary equipment and added more armour.

Night fighter variant

In an effort to improve night-fighting capability, the Bf 110E-1/U-1 added an early infrared sensor as an airborne interception aid; it proved disappointing in service. In 1941 examples of the Bf 110E-1/U1 were delivered to a Staffel of I./ Nachtjagdgeschwader 1 based at Venlo, and these were equipped with an experimental version of the Lichtenstein BC (FuG 202) air interception (AI) radar which had a

maximum range of 3.5km (2.2 miles) and a minimum range of 200m (655ft); it was not until July 1942, however, that AI radar was issued as standard to frontline units, in the form of the Lichtenstein C-1 (FuG 212). The Bf 110E-1/U2 was the next night fighter derivative and the first to add a third crewmember.

Bf 110F series

The Bf 110F was generally similar to the E-series but introduced a new powerplant in the form of the 1007kW (1350hp) DB 601F-1 engine. In its initial Bf 110F-1 form the aircraft was optimized for close support with standard gun armament, two ETC 500 and four ETC 50 bomb racks, plus additional armour including a protected windshield. The Bf 110F-2 was a heavy fighter derivative without the ETC racks, while the Bf 110E-3 was the reconnaissance equivalent.

The F-series was built in subvariants up to and including the Bf 110F-4 that became a standard night fighter. The F-4 was powered by a pair of DB 601F-1 engines and armed with a pair of 20mm (0.8in) MG FF/M cannon and four 7.92mm (0.31in) MG 17 machine guns in the nose; as an option, two

This tropicalised Bf 110E-1 was operated by 8./ Zerstörergeschwader 26 from Derna, Libya, in September 1942. The individual aircraft letter in red signified an aircraft assigned to the 8. Staffel.

Messerschmitt Bf 110E-1

Weight (Maximum take-off) 6750kg (14,881lb)

Dimensions Length: 12.1m (39ft 8in), Wingspan: 16.2m (53ft 2in), Height: 3.5m (11ft 6in)

Powerplant Two 895kW (1200hp) Daimler-Benz DB 601N-1 12 cylinder inverted-V type engine

Speed 560km/h (349mph)

Range 775km (482 miles)

Ceiling 8000m (26,245ft)

Crew 2

Armament Two 20mm (0.8in) MG FF/M cannon, four 7.92mm (0.31in) MG 17 machine guns, one 7.92mm (0.31in) MG 15 machine gun; four ETC 50 bomb racks under the wings for a bombload up to 1200kg (2645lb)

30mm (1.18in) MK 108 cannon could replace the MG FF/M, and were carried in a ventral tray. Other changes included improved UV instrument lighting and radio equipment.

The radar-equipped Bf 110F-4a (FuG 202) was additionally provided with the option of a pair of 300-litre

Messerschmitt Bf 110F-1

This Bf 110F-1 was operated by II./
Zerstörergeschwader 26 serving on the Eastern
Front in 1942.

Messerschmitt Bf 110F-1

Weight (Maximum take-off) 6750kg (14,881lb)

Dimensions Length: 12.1m (39ft 8in), Wingspan:
16.27m (53ft 4in), Height: 3.5m (11ft 6in)

Powerplant Two 1007kW (1350hp) DB 601F-1
inverted-V type engine

Speed 560km/h (349mph)

Range 775km (482 miles)

Ceiling 8000m (26,245ft)

Crew 2

Armament Two 20mm (0.8in) MG FF/M cannon,
four 7.92mm (0.31in) MG 17 machine guns, one
7.92mm (0.31in) MG 15 machine gun; two ETC 500
and four ETC 50 bomb racks

(66-Imp gal) drop tanks underwing,
flame-dampers and night glimmer
high-explosive ammunition. It featured
revised armament, with the 20mm
(0.8in) MG FF/Ms replaced by twin
20mm Mauser MG 151/20 weapons.

In 1943 the night fighter units also
began to arm their aircraft with a pair
of 20mm (0.8in) MG FF/M cannons
installed in the aft cockpit and angled

at 60–70 degrees from the horizontal –
the upwards-firing installation was
known as *Schräge Musik* ('jazz music')
and produced the Bf 110F-4/U1
subvariant.

Messerschmitt Bf 110G

**Introduction of the 1100kW (1475hp) DB 605B-1 engines created the next and final
major production series, the Bf 110G, built in subvariants up to and including the
Bf 110G-4.**

The initial series-production model
was the Bf 110G-1, a heavy day fighter
with an armament of twin 20mm (0.8in)
MG 151/20 cannon and four 7.92mm
(0.31in) MG 17 machine guns in the
nose. Revised vertical tail surfaces
and strengthened undercarriage
characterised the Bf 110G-2, which
was the next fighter/close support
version with ETC 250 and ETC 50/
VIII racks or 300-litre (66-Imp gal)
underwing drop tanks. This subvariant
also introduced a twin 7.92mm
(0.31in) MG 81Z machine gun for
the rear gunner.

Further iterations of the Bf 110G
comprised the Bf 110G-2/R1 bomber

destroyer with a single 37mm (1.45in)
BK 3,7 cannon in a belly tray and with
the 20mm (0.8in) cannon removed.
The Bf 110G-2/R2 was similar but with
provision for GM-1 power-boosting,
while the Bf 110G-2/R3 was a heavy
fighter version with twin 30mm (1.18in)
MK 108 cannon in place of the four
nose-mounted machine guns; the MG
151/20 cannon were retained. The
Bf 110G-3 was the next in the line of
reconnaissance variants.

Bf 110G-4 night fighter
The definitive night fighter was
the Bf 110G-4, initially equipped
with Lichtenstein C-1 (FuG 212) air

interception (AI) radar; in this form it
was known as the Bf 110G-4a. The
armament now reverted to the previous
twin MG 151/20 cannon and four MG
17 machine guns. Once the Royal
Air Force began to employ Window
countermeasures, the night fighter's
equipment was revised to include the
Lichtenstein SN-2 (FuG 220) radar; as
of late 1943, the SN-2-equipped Bf
110G-4b was the mainstay of the night
fighter arm.

By June 1944, the Bf 110G-4 was
being operated by the majority of
Gruppen within Nachtjagdgeschwader
1, 3, 4, 5 and 6, which provided
a defensive chain stretching from

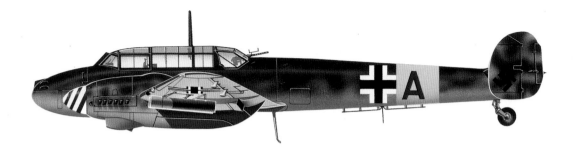

Aalborg in Denmark to Reims in France, and from Schleissheim in Bavaria to the Romanian border. Among Bf 110 night fighter pilots, the leading exponent was Major Heinz-Wolfgang Schnaufer, the final *Kommodore* of NJG 4, and the top-scoring night fighter pilot of World War II, who claimed 121 nocturnal kills during the conflict.

Once in service, the Bf 110G-4a night fighter was provided with a range of different field modification (*Rüstsätze*) kits. These included the Bf 110G-4a/R1 with a single 37mm (1.46in) BK 3,7 cannon, the Bf 110G-4a/R2 with GM-1 boosting and the Bf 110G-4a/R3 with twin 30mm (1.18in) MK 108s replacing the MG 17s.

The next subvariants were the Bf 110G-4b night fighter with the FuG 220 radar (the FuG 212 was retained for close-range work) and the Bf 110G-4c night fighter with improved FuG 220B and various different *Rüstsätze* options for weapons, fuel tanks and GM-1 equipment.

Bf 110H subvariant

Planned as the last of the line was the Bf 110H – essentially similar to the G-series – the final subvariant of which would have been the Bf 110H-4. In the event, the H-series was manufactured only in small numbers and in parallel with the Bf 110G. The

Messerschmitt Bf 110G-2

This Bf 110G-2 flew with 5./Zerstörergeschwader 76 (ZG 76) at Grosenhain, during the winter of 1943–44.

only significant difference was the powerplant, the H-series substituting the DB 605E for the DB 605B used in the Bf 110G family.

By the time production was complete, around 6050 Bf 110s of all variants had been manufactured, with the last examples coming off the production lines as late as March 1945.

Messerschmitt Bf 110G-2

Weight (Maximum take-off) 6750kg (14,881lb)

Dimensions Length: 12.65m (41ft 6in), Wingspan: 16.27m (53ft 4in), Height: 3.5m (11ft 6in)

Powerplant Two 1100kW (1475hp) DB 605 12-cylinder inverted-V engines

Speed 560km/h (349mph)

Range 775km (482 miles)

Ceiling 10,900m (35,760ft)

Crew 2/3

Armament Two 20mm (0.8in) MG 151/20 cannon, four 7.92mm (0.31in) MG 17 machine guns, twin 7.92mm (0.31in) MG 18Z machine guns (rear cockpit); provision for ETC 250 and ETC 50/VIII racks or 300-litre (66-Imp gal) underwing drop tanks

The Lichtenstein BC radar improved the chances of a Bf 110 detecting a bomber at night, but it reduced by around 40km/h (25mph) the aircraft's top speed.

Messerschmitt Bf 110G-4b/R3

This Bf 110F-4b night fighter was flown by Wilhelm Johnen of 5./NJG 5, in April 1944. The aircraft strayed
into Switzerland and was forced to land near Lake Constance, where Johnen and his crew were interned.

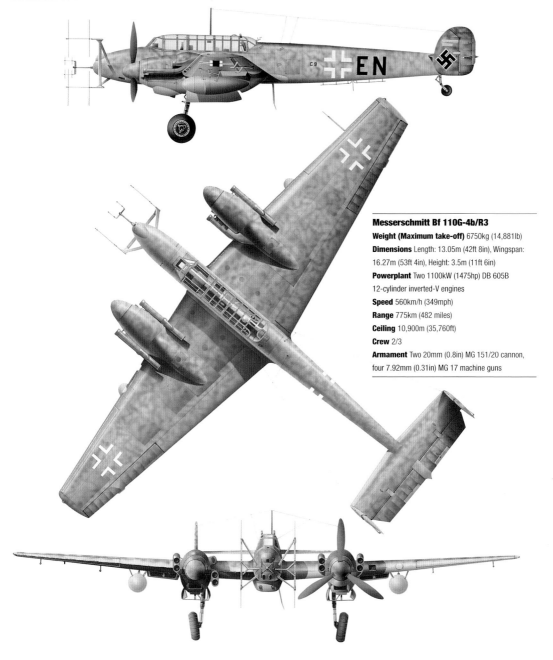

Messerschmitt Bf 110G-4b/R3

Weight (Maximum take-off) 6750kg (14,881lb)

Dimensions Length: 13.05m (42ft 8in), Wingspan:
16.27m (53ft 4in), Height: 3.5m (11ft 6in)

Powerplant Two 1100kW (1475hp) DB 605B
12-cylinder inverted-V engines

Speed 560km/h (349mph)

Range 775km (482 miles)

Ceiling 10,900m (35,760ft)

Crew 2/3

Armament Two 20mm (0.8in) MG 151/20 cannon,
four 7.92mm (0.31in) MG 17 machine guns

Messerschmitt Bf 110G-4/R3

Night fighter squadron 2./Nachtjagdgeschwader 5 operated from Dreux, France, in 1944. This was a Bf 110G-4/R3 sub-variant with two MG 151s under the belly, two MK 108s in the nose, two optional upward-firing MG FF in a *Schräge Musik* installation, plus a twin MG 81Z in the rear of the cockpit.

Focke-Wulf Fw 187 *Falke*

Devised by Kurt Tank, the Fw 187 *Falke* ('falcon') was a twin-engine single-seat day fighter of all-metal construction that was originally schemed as a private venture in 1936.

The aircraft was based around a powerplant of the Daimler Benz DB 600 engine, which was then in development; detail design was handled by Tank's assistant, Rudolf Blaser. The project found favour with the *Reichsluftfahrtministerium* (RLM, German Air Ministry), which requested three prototypes be completed.

The resulting aircraft featured an exceptionally narrow fuselage, the dimensions of which dictated that certain pilot instruments had to be installed on the inboard sections of the engine cowlings, from where they could be seen by the pilot.

With the planned DB 600 engines in short supply, the RLM permitted Focke-Wulf to complete the first prototype, the Fw 187 V1, with Jumo 210 engines instead. In this form, the initial prototype completed its maiden flight in late spring 1937, with test pilot Hans Sander in the cockpit. Despite the limited power output of the Jumo engines – 507kW (680hp) each

– the initial prototype demonstrated impressive performance, including a speed of 523km/h (325mph) compared with the 560km/h (348mph) that had been envisaged for the DB 600-engined fighter. The prototype underwent a series of refinements as it was tested, including replacement of the Junkers-Hamilton variable-pitch propellers with VDM units, twin wheels on each main landing gear leg and a single 7.92mm (0.31in) MG 17 machine gun installed on each side of the cockpit.

New prototypes

The Fw 187 V1 was lost in an accident in May 1938, but a second prototype, the Fw 187 V2, had taken to the air in the summer of 1937, powered by Jumo 210Ga engines and with a rudder of reduced chord.

The third aircraft, the Fw 187 V3, was completed as a two-seat interdictor, with a redesigned fuselage that included longer engine bearers,

Focke-Wulf Fw 187 Falke A-0

Weight (Maximum take-off) 5000kg (11,023lb)
Dimensions Length: 11.1m (36ft 5in), Wingspan: 15.3m (50ft 2in), Height: 3.85m (12ft 8in)
Powerplant Two 507kW (680hp) Junkers Jumo 210Ga V-12 liquid-cooled piston engines
Speed 523km/h (325mph)
Time to altitude 6000m (19,685ft) in 5 minutes 48 seconds
Ceiling 10,000m (33,000ft)
Crew 2
Armament Four 7.92mm (0.31in) MG 17 machine guns in fuselage sides, two 20mm (0.8in) MG FF cannon in lower fuselage

plus revised engine nacelles and full-span flaps. It was armed with a pair of 20mm (0.8in) MG FF cannon and first flew in spring 1938. Another two prototypes were completed to a similar standard.

Despite the loss of the first prototype, the programme continued. The sixth prototype, the Fw 187

V6, was provided with a pair of 746kW (1000hp) DB 600A engines and achieved a speed of 636km/h (395mph). Although three pre-production Fw 189A-0 aircraft were built, armed with four MG 17 machine guns and two 20mm (0.8in) MG FF cannon, no quantity production was authorised, the Luftwaffe unconvinced there was a role for an 'intermediate' fighter between the single-engine Bf 109 and the twin-engine Bf 110

heavy fighter. As it was, the pre-production machines were used to defend the Focke-Wulf factory at Bremen in summer 1940, forming a so-called *Industrie-Schutzstaffel* (industry defence squadron), before being passed to 13.(Zerstörer) Staffel of Jagdgeschwader 77 in Norway, which continued to operate them on an ad-hoc basis. Another example served with the Luftwaffe aerial gunnery school in Værløse, Denmark in 1942.

Focke-Wulf Fw 187 Falke

This pre-production Fw 187 *Falke* was likely assigned to the Focke-Wulf factory in Bremen for airfield defence in 1940.

A front view of the twin-engined Focke-Wulf Fw 187, January 1940.

Dornier Do 17 night fighter

Emerging in 1933 from an original Deutsche Lufthansa requirement for a high-speed six-passenger mailplane, the Dornier Do 17 was a shoulder-wing, all-metal, twin-engine monoplane that entered military service as a medium bomber.

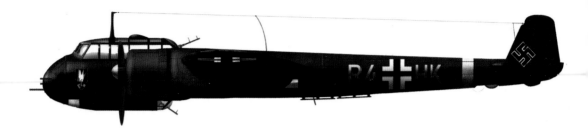

Dornier Do 17Z-7 Kauz I

R4+HK was flown by 2./Nachtjagdgeschwader 2, based at Gilze-Rijen in the Netherlands in November 1940.

The Do 17 was not necessarily an ideal platform for a night fighter but it came to be used in the role primarily because large numbers of surplus airframes were becoming available after they began to be withdrawn from frontline service as bombers. The impetus to create a night fighter arm was provided by the British Royal Air Force launching nocturnal raids against Germany in May 1940.

Without adequate defensive measures in place, the Luftwaffe rushed to respond with, initially, a force of adapted Messerschmitt Bf 110s and Junkers Ju 88Cs. However, consideration was also given to converting other light bombers to the night fighter role, including the Do 17.

Do 17Z

The primary night fighter versions of the Do 17 were based on the most prolific Do 17Z, of which around 1700 examples were completed between 1939 and 1940. The initial Do 17Z-0 had been powered by two Bramo 323A-1 engines developing

671kW (900hp) each, replaced by 746kW (1000hp) Bramo 323P engines replacing the Bramo 323A-1s in the Do 17Z-2.

The first of the resulting night fighter versions was the one-off Do 17Z-6 *Kauz* I ('screech owl' I), developed as a long-range intruder and night fighter and incorporating the nose of the Junkers Ju 88C-2 that was fitted with a forward-firing armament of one 20mm (0.8in) MG FF cannon and three 7.92mm (0.31in) MG 17 machine guns. This nose was grafted onto the existing fuselage of a Do 17Z-3 – a reconnaissance version of the Z-series. The result was considered unsatisfactory, and no quantity production was undertaken.

Dedicated night fighter

The Do 17Z-10 *Kauz* II was a dedicated night fighter with a forward-firing armament of two MG FF cannon and four MG 17 machine guns in an entirely new, purpose-designed nose. Aerial interception equipment consisted of the Spanner-II-Anlage infrared

Dornier Do 17Z-7 Kauz I

Weight (Maximum take-off) 7300kg (16,100lb)

Dimensions Length: 15.8m (51ft 10in), Wingspan: 18m (59ft 1in), Height: 4.56m (15ft)

Powerplant Two 746kW (1000hp) Bramo 323P-1 radial engines

Speed 410km/h (255mph)

Range 660km (410 miles)

Ceiling 8200m (26,900ft)

Crew 4

Armament One 20mm (0.8in) MG FF cannon and three 7.92mm (0.31in) MG 17 machine guns

detection aid. The Spanner-II-Anlage was a passive detection system that sensed hot exhaust pipes and flames; it superseded the Spanner-I active detection device that used a 1kW lap to project an infrared beam and a detector to sense any targets.

A total of nine Do 17Z-10 aircraft were completed. At least one example of the *Kauz* II was also tested with the Lichtenstein C1 airborne interception radar, but this wasn't a standard feature. In both the Do 17Z-6 and Z-10, the crew complement was reduced to three, with the flight engineer responsible for loading the MG FF weapons and the radio operator firing the aft-facing defensive machine guns.

Combat record

The first of several Do 17Z-10 kills was recorded on the night of 16/17 October 1940 by Ludwig Becker of 4./Nachtjagdgeschwader 1, based at Deelen in the Netherlands, who downed an RAF Wellington bomber

Dornier Do 17Z-10 Kauz II
Do 17Z-10 R4+GK was flown by 2./ Nachtjagdgeschwader 2 from Gilze-Rijen in spring May 1941. This aircraft was shot down by an RAF Beaufighter on the night of 7/8 May 1941, coming down near Carrington, Lincolnshire.

over the Zuiderzee. He had been guided to within 50m (164ft) of the target under ground-based radar control – the first such victory of the war for the Luftwaffe.

The Do 17Z night fighter variants were only ever an interim solution, however, and by the end of that year the type was being replaced in this role by the Dornier Do 215B.

Dornier Do 17Z-10 Kauz II
R4+LK was another of 2./Nachtjagdgeschwader 2's Do 17Z-10s, based at Gilze-Rijen in November 1941. It was the first of the unit's aircraft to be damaged in combat, engaging with an enemy night fighter while being flown by *Oberfeldwebel* Herbert Schmidt on 9 November 1940.

Dornier Do 17Z-10 Kauz II
Weight (Maximum take-off) 7300kg (16,100lb)
Dimensions Length: 15.8m (51ft 10in), Wingspan: 18m (59ft 1in), Height: 4.56m (15ft)
Powerplant Two 746kW (1000hp) Bramo 323P-1 radial engines
Speed 410km/h (255mph)
Range 660km (410 miles)
Ceiling 8200m (26,900ft)
Crew 3
Armament Two 20mm (0.8in) MG FF cannon and four 7.92mm (0.31in) MG 17 machine guns

Dornier Do 215 night fighter

The Dornier Do 215 was developed originally as an export-optimized Do 17Z medium bomber/reconnaissance aircraft.

Dornier Do 215B-5 Kauz III

R4+DC was an aircraft of the Stab. II/Nachtjagdgeschwader 2 based at Leeuwarden in the Netherlands in summer 1942. Visible under the forward fuselage is a weapons tray which increased total forward-firing armament to four MG 17s and two MG/FF cannon.

It was initially ordered by Sweden, in the shape of the Do 215A-1 that was powered by a pair of 802kW (1075hp) Daimler-Benz DB 601A inverted-Vee engines. However, the 18 aircraft intended for Sweden were embargoed by Germany during the production phase and redirected to the Luftwaffe, which introduced them to service as the Do 215B-0 pre-production aircraft and Do 215B-1 production aircraft – both were outfitted for long-range reconnaissance and entered service in January 1940.

There was also a pair of Do 215B-3 aircraft delivered to the Soviet Union in 1940, while the Do 215B-4 was equipped for bomber-reconnaissance duties and entered Luftwaffe service in March 1940.

Night intruder

As production and service of the Do 215B for the Luftwaffe continued, the limited success achieved by the Do 17Z-10 *Kauz* II suggested that a comparable conversion from Do 215B standard could produce a Luftwaffe

night fighter with usefully higher performance than the *Kauz* II. The latter's indifferent speed made it better suited to the offensive night-intruder mission than to the defensive night-interceptor role.

In late autumn 1940, work was undertaken to convert the Do 215B-4 to a similar configuration as the Do 17Z-10 night fighter/intruder, resulting in the Do 215B-5 – sometimes known as the *Kauz* III ('screech owl' III). In terms of weaponry, it shared the fixed forward-firing armament of two 20mm (0.8in) MG FF cannon and four 7.92mm (0.31in) MG 17 machine guns with the Do 17Z-10; the machine guns were installed in a solid nose that replaced the previous glazed bombardier nose, while the cannon were located in the lower nose.

The nose cone also housed the Spanner-Anlage infrared detection aid that was used to detect the heat plumes of enemy bombers' engine exhausts. In operational use, the Spanner-Anlage proved to be oversensitive, unreliable and

Dornier Do-215 B-5 Kauz III

Weight (Maximum take-off) 6800kg (14,991lb)

Dimensions Length: 15.8m (51ft 10in), Wingspan: 18m (59ft 1in), Height: 4.56m (15ft)

Powerplant Two 802kW (1075hp) Daimler-Benz DB 601A inverted-Vee engines

Speed 470km/h (290mph)

Range 380km (240 miles)

Ceiling 9000m (30,000ft)

Crew 3

Armament Two 20mm (0.8in) MG FF cannon (nose), four 7.92mm (0.31in) MG 17 machine guns (nose), one 7.92mm (0.31in) MG 17 machine gun (rear cockpit)

only effective over short distances;
furthermore, it was unable to provide
any directional information on
potential targets.

Therefore, the Do 215B-5 was
adapted to carry the Lichtenstein
BC (FuG 202) airborne interception
radar, replacing the Spanner-Anlage.
This paved the way for subsequent
installation of the radar in the
Messerschmitt Bf 110 and
Junkers Ju 88 night fighters.

In the Do 215B-5, the Lichtenstein
BC installation included a *Matraze*
('mattress') array of four 'stag's horn'
antennas on the extreme nose to
provide detection of targets at a range
of between 200m and 4000m (656ft
and 13,123ft) as well as the target's
bearing in azimuth and elevation.
The radar was initially installed in a
Do 215B-4 on an experimental basis,
before being standardised on the
definitive Do 215B-5 night fighter.
The installation of the radar reduced
the aircraft's maximum speed by
25km/h (15.5mph), as a result of drag
produced by the radar antennas.

Combat record

The first examples of the Do
215B-5 were delivered to 4./
Nachtjagdgeschwader 2 in spring
1941 and these aircraft were initially
used for intruder sorties over British
bomber bases. In this role the Do
215B-5 proved initially successful, with
a total of 18 Royal Air Force bombers

lost to intruders between April and
June 1941.

A first radar-aided kill by the type
was achieved on the night of 8/9
August 1941, by pilot Ludwig Becker,
who had also been responsible for
the first Do 17Z-10 kill. Becker and
his radio operator Josef Staub were
the first Luftwaffe night fighter crew
to intercept an enemy bomber using
airborne radar, using the Lichtenstein
BC to track an RAF Wellington bomber
that was downed near Bunde. Becker
added further aerial victories to his
tally and had achieved five kills by 2
October, becoming the Luftwaffe's first
night fighter ace.

Nachtjagdgeschwader 2
Established in September 1940 at Gilze-Rijen, from sub-units
of Nachtjagdgeschwader 1 (NJG 1) and Zerstörergeschwader
2 (ZG 2), NJG 2 initially carried out long-range intruder missions
over the UK. Operations commenced using Ju 88C-1s,
although a handful of Do 215B-5s were trialled in spring 1941.
By October 1941, night-intruder sorties had been wound
up and that November, 4./NJG 2 moved to Catania, Sicily,
where it remained until February 1942. In November 1941, 2./
NJG 2 moved to Benghazi while returning to Catania later that month. Early in
1942 both 2. and 3./NJG 2 were based at Benghazi until March 1942. From
April onwards, I./NJG 2 was scattered over the Mediterranean, with various
detachments. By the end of 1944, NJG 2 was providing night defence of the
industrial Ruhr area, flying from Düsseldorf, Kassel, Gütersloh, and Cologne.

Other notable pilots to have flown the Do 215B-5 included Helmut Lent, who was eventually credited with 110 aircraft shot down, with 102 of them at night.

Do 215B-5

As a result of this early success, further production ensued, with aircraft now being issued to I, III and IV./NJG 1 and I and II./NJG 2 later the same year. At least 20 of the Do 215B-5s were eventually completed, most if not all based on conversions of the final Do 215B-4 aircraft on the production line. Fortunately for the RAF, the value of the intruder operations was not obvious to everyone within the Luftwaffe's high command and opposition to them arose. They were eventually stopped on 10 October 1941 on direct orders from Hitler.

This, combined with a limited production run, ensured that the Do 215B-5 would remain an interim night fighter, but it paved the way for the subsequent development of the Do 217J and N, which were built in greater numbers and a greater diversity of variants.

Dornier Do 215B-5 Kauz III

R4+AP was a Do 215B-5 serving with 6./Nachtjagdgeschwader 2 at Leeuwarden in 1941. *Oberleutnant* Ludwig Becker was flying this aircraft when it downed an RAF Manchester east-northeast of Enkhuizen, early in the morning of 9 March 1942.

Dornier Do 215B-5 Kauz III

R4+SN was another Leeuwarden-based Kauz III, belonging to 5./Nachtjagdgeschwader 2 in spring 1942. Among its pilots was *Hauptmann* Paul Gildner.

Dornier Do-215 B-5 Kauz III

Weight (Maximum take-off) 6800kg (14,991lb)
Dimensions Length: 15.8m (51ft 10in), Wingspan: 18m (59ft 1in), Height: 4.56m (15ft)
Powerplant Two 802kW (1075hp) Daimler-Benz DB 601A inverted-Vee engines
Speed 470km/h (290mph)
Range 380km (240 miles)
Ceiling 9000m (30,000ft)
Crew 3
Armament Two 20mm (0.8in) MG FF cannon and four 7.92mm (0.31in) MG 17 machine guns

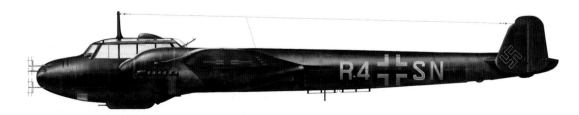

Dornier Do 217 night fighter

The ultimate night fighter versions of the Dornier twin-engine bombers were based on the airframe of the Do 217. This aircraft began life as an enlarged and further refined Do 17 and entered Luftwaffe service as the Do 217E in 1940.

The first of the Do 217 night fighter line was the Do 217J-1, a radarless night intruder that began to be delivered to the Luftwaffe in summer 1942. This was proposed by Dornier in early 1941, despite the fact that the basic aircraft – already considerably heavier than the Do 17 – lacked the 1491kW (2000hp) engines that were required for it to meet its performance targets.

The primary change in the J-series was the introduction of a 'solid' nose in place of the previous multi-panel Plexiglass unit for the bomb-aimer. The new nose housed four 20mm (08in) MG FF cannon and four 7.92mm (0.31in) MG 17 machine guns. The aft defensive armament was inherited from the Do 217E-2 and comprised a 13mm (0.51in) MG 131 machine gun in a dorsal turret and a hand-aimed MG 13 in the ventral position.

Do 217J-1 operational

The initial Do 217J-1 became operational in February 1942 and was followed by the Do 217J-2 night fighter, now with Lichtenstein BC (FuG 202) radar. Other equipment fielded once in service included Flensburg and Naxos, which were designed to

Dornier Do 217J-1

Wearing one of the more exotic schemes applied to a Dornier twin, Do 217J-1 KD+MZ was assigned to Nachtjagdgeschwader 4 in December 1942.

home in on Royal Air Force bomber radar emissions.

The Do 217J-2 is thought to have completed a maiden flight in spring 1942. The bomb bays of the Do 217J-1 night intruder were deleted and the J-2 was also lighter than previous versions; despite the introduction of the *Matraze* (mattress) array of antennas on the nose, performance remained similar.

Examples of the Do 217J-2 served in small numbers with Nachtjagdgeschwader 1 and 2, while NJG 3 and III./NJG 4 were both fully equipped with the type. However, only limited combat operations were undertaken prior to 1943. With the end of night intruder missions over the UK in October 1941, the Do 217J was only flown over Germany and, from September 1942, was operated by the Italian air force in the Mediterranean theatre.

Crews appreciated the firepower and long endurance of the Do 217J,

Dornier Do 217J-1

Weight (Maximum take-off) 10,950kg (24,140lb)
Dimensions Length: 17.67m (57ft 11in), Wingspan: 19m (62ft 4in), Height: 4.8m (15ft 8in)
Powerplant Two 1147kW (1539hp) BMW 801ML piston radial engines
Speed 489km/h (304mph)
Range 2180km (1350 miles)
Ceiling 9500m (31,200ft)
Crew 4
Armament Four 20mm (0.8in) MG FF cannon and four 7.92mm (0.31in) MG 17 machine guns (nose); one 13mm (0.51in) MG 131 machine gun (dorsal turret) and one 7.92mm (0.31in) MG 13 (ventral position)

but it lacked agility and its weight limited the number of airfields from which it could operate.

The final variant to see quantity production was the Do 217N, with a Daimler-Benz powerplant. An initial Do 217N took to the air on 31 July 1942, powered by DB 603A engines rated at 1305kW (1750hp) for take-off and 1380kW (1850hp) at 2100m (6890ft); flame-dampers were routinely fitted. Production Do 217N-1 aircraft began to be delivered to the Luftwaffe in January 1943. The Do 217N-1/US subvariant was often equipped to carry four 20mm (0.8in) cannon in an upward-firing *Schräge Musik* installation, but its speed was limited to 525km/h (326mph).

Do 217N-2

By mid-1943, production had switched to the Do 217N-2 that had the dorsal turret and lower rear gun gondola removed and replaced with wooden

Dornier Do 217J-2

G8+HM was assigned to 2./Nachtjagdgeschwader 1 at Leeuwarden in autumn 1942.

fairings. This trimmed off 2 tonnes of weight and reduced drag, boosting maximum speed at medium altitude to over 500km/h (310mph). Forward-firing armament comprised four MG 151/20 cannon and four MG 17s, and another four MG 151s were arranged to fire at 70 degrees upwards in a *Schräge Musik* installation. The Do 217N-2 was also soon provided with Lichtenstein SN-2 radar.

Among the pilots to fly the Do 217 in the night fighter role was Rudolf Schönert, who pioneered the use of the *Schräge Musik* armament while serving with NJG 1 in early 1943.

Around 200 Do 217Ns were eventually completed and these served with NJG 3 and NJG 4, as well as II./NJG 2 and III./NJG 2 in the Mediterranean theatre in

Dornier Do 217J-2

Weight (Maximum take-off) 10,950kg (24,140lb)

Dimensions Length: 17.67m (57ft 11in), Wingspan: 19m (62ft 4in), Height: 4.8m (15ft 8in)

Powerplant Two 1147kW (1539hp) BMW 801ML piston radial engines

Speed 489km/h (304mph)

Range 2180km (1350 miles)

Ceiling 9500m (31,200ft)

Crew 4

Armament Four 20mm (0.8in) MG 151 cannon and four 7.92mm (0.31in) MG 17 machine guns (nose); one 13mm (0.51in) MG 131 machine gun (dorsal turret) and one 7.92mm (0.31in) MG 13 (ventral position)

The Do 217J-2 was equipped with FuG radar, and entered service in small numbers from late 1942.

1943. However, production came at considerable cost and disruption to the bomber manufacturing effort and it was decided to discontinue production in mid-1943 in favour of night fighter variants of the Bf 110 and Ju 88.

Wide deployment

As of 1944, Do 217Js and Ns remained in use with a wide variety of Luftwaffe units, equipping around 10 Gruppen, as well as serving on the Eastern Front with I./NJG 100. Despite the powerful armament of the Do 217 night fighters, these aircraft continued to lack performance, and as a result the type was increasingly used as fighter

Dornier Do 217N-1

Do 217N-1 3C+DV was operated by II./Nachtjagdgeschwader 4 from a base in Germany in late 1943.

controller, employing its own radar to guide more agile Messerschmitt Bf 110s to bomber targets. Within mixed-type night fighter groups, Do 217s were typically assigned to the most junior crews, while the more experienced pilots preferred to fly the Bf 110 or Junkers Ju 88.

From a total of 364 Do 217Js and Do 217Ns completed, almost all had been removed from the frontline inventory by mid-1944.

Dornier Do 217N-1

Weight (Maximum take-off) 15,000kg (33,000lb)

Dimensions Length: 17.67m (57ft 11in), Wingspan: 19m (62ft 4in), Height: 4.8m (15ft 8in)

Powerplant Two 1380kW (1850hp) DB 603A piston V12 aircraft engine

Speed 525km/h (326mph)

Range 1755km (1090 miles)

Ceiling 8400m (27,600ft)

Crew 4

Armament Four 20mm (0.8in) MG 151 cannon and four 7.92mm (0.31in) MG 17 machine guns (nose); one 13mm (0.51in) MG 131 machine gun (dorsal turret) and one 7.92mm (0.31in) MG 13 (ventral position)

The heavy armament of the Do 217 series is obvious on the nose of this N2, with four cannon and four machine guns, as well as the antennas of the FuG 212 Lichtenstein C-1 radar.

Junkers Ju 88C heavy fighters

While it had initially been developed as a bomber, such was the speed of the twin-engine Ju 88 that thought soon turned to creating a fighter version that would exploit the performance and manoeuvrability of the basic design.

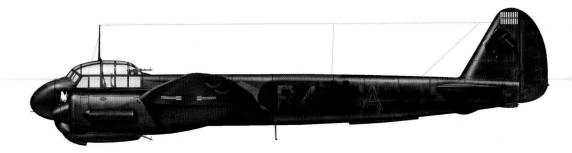

Junkers Ju 88C-4
Weight (Maximum take-off) 12,105kg (26,686lb)
Dimensions Length: 14.96m (49ft), Wingspan: 20.08m (65ft 9in), Height: 5m (16ft 7in)
Powerplant Two 990kW (1320hp) Jumo 211F piston V-12 engines
Speed 480km/h (300mph)
Range 1789km (1112 miles)
Ceiling 9600m (31,500ft)
Crew 3
Armament One 20mm (0.8in) MG FF cannon and three 7.92mm (0.31in) MG 17 machine guns (nose), two MG FF cannon (ventral gondola), one rear-firing 13mm (0.51in) MG 131 machine gun

Junkers Ju 88C-4
Ju 88C-4 R4+AC was an aircraft of the Stab II/. Nachtjagdgeschwader 2, piloted by *Hauptmann* Dr Horst Patuschka at Comiso, Sicily, in 1943.

This emerged as the Ju 88C *Zerstörer* (heavy fighter) series, which was first flown in prototype form in summer 1939. The initial aircraft was the modified Ju 88 V7 prototype, fitted with a 20mm (0.8in) MG FF cannon and three 7.92mm (0.31in) MG 17 machine guns firing through panels in the nose. A first production *Zerstörer* subvariant was to have been the Ju 88C-1 that was based on the Ju 88B airframe and powered by a pair of BMW 139 radial engines, later switched to BMW 801MA units. However, the demand for these powerplants for the Focke-Wulf Fw 190 production effort saw the project abandoned.

Ju 88A-1 conversion
Instead, the initial production version reverted to the Jumo 211 powerplant and became the Ju 88C-2, a conversion of the Ju 88A-1 on the production line that incorporated a solid nose accommodating an MG FF cannon and three MG 17 machine guns. Defensive armament consisted of two further 7.92mm (0.31in) MG 15 machine guns.

Only a small number of Ju 88C-2s were completed and these also featured armour and retained the Ju 88A-1's aft bomb bay. These aircraft were mainly used for anti-shipping work with Zerst./ Kampfgeschwader 30 and on night intruder missions over Britain with II./ Nachtjagdgeschwader 1 until October 1941. Thereafter, they were flown in the Mediterranean theatre.

Ju 88C-4
The Ju 88C-4 was a heavy fighter/ reconnaissance subvariant that was built as such, rather than being produced through conversion. It featured the long-span wing and Jumo 211F/J powerplant of the Ju 88A-4 bomber. Armament was boosted with two more MG FF cannon in a ventral gondola, which could also be configured with cameras for

reconnaissance. Additional guns could be carried in underwing pods.

A further improved heavy fighter appeared in the form of the Ju 88C-5, powered by BMW 801 engines but used only for trials work, before being refined to create the Ju 88C-6. This became the major production version, coming out of the factory from early 1942, and featuring improved armour protection but otherwise similar to the Ju 88C-4.

Among the more important roles conducted by this variant was anti-shipping on behalf of Kampfgeschwader 40 from bases in France, as well as efforts to intercept Allied aircraft being ferried at night to North Africa. Another role for the Ju 88C-6C was 'train-busting' on the Eastern Front, a task that began to be conducted from early 1943.

Intruder version

Intruder versions of the Ju 88 fighter included the Ju 88C-7a with a ventral cannon tray and the similar Ju 88C-7b that featured underwing bomb racks. The final major production derivative was another heavy fighter, the Ju 88C-7c, with BMW 801 engines and 20mm (0.8in) MG 151/20 cannon in the nose. Ultimately, around 3200 Ju 88Cs were produced.

Mention should also be made of the Ju 88G-10, a long-range *Zerstörer*

Junkers Ju 88C-6

With national markings obscured, this Ju 88C-6 *Zerstörer* served with V./Kampfgeschwader 40 against Allied anti-submarine aircraft and as an escort fighter for the Focke-Wulf Fw 200 Condor maritime patrol aircraft.

that was based on the airframe of the Ju 88G night fighter. This featured a stretched fuselage containing additional fuel but the small number that were completed were ultimately directed to the *Mistel* composite aircraft programme.

The day fighter Ju 88C-6 packed a heavy punch in the form of three 20mm (0./8in) cannon and three 7.92mm (0.31in) machine guns.

Junkers Ju 88C-6

Weight (Maximum take-off) 12,105kg (26,686lb)

Dimensions Length: 14.96m (49ft), Wingspan: 20.08m (65ft 9in), Height: 5m (16ft 7in)

Powerplant Two 1044kW (1401hp) Jumo 211J piston V-12 engines

Speed 480km/h (300mph)

Range 1789km (1112 miles)

Ceiling 9900m (32,480ft)

Crew 3

Armament One 20mm (0.8in) MG FF cannon and three 7.92mm (0.31in) MG 17 machine guns (nose), two 20mm (0.8in) MG 151/20 cannon (ventral gondola), one rear-firing 13mm (0.51in) MG 131 machine gun

---

Junkers Ju 88 night fighters

The Royal Air Force's increasing nocturnal bombing raids on Germany had led to an urgent requirement for a night fighter by mid-1940.

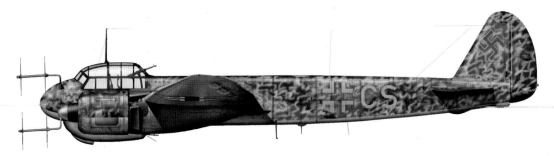

The first radar-equipped, Jumo-engined Ju 88C-6b night fighters began to appear in late 1942, these being based on the airframe of the Ju 88C-6 heavy fighter. The Ju 88C-6b

Junkers Ju 88G-1

Weight (Maximum take-off) 12,100kg (26,675lb)
Dimensions Length: 15.50m (50ft 9in), Wingspan: 20.08m (65ft 9in), Height: 5.07m (16ft 7in)
Powerplant Two 1250kW (1677hp) BMW 801MA piston radial engines
Speed 540km/h (335mph)
Range 2800km (1739 miles)
Ceiling 9400m (30,840ft)
Crew 4
Armament Six 20mm (0.8in) MG 151/20 cannon (two in the nose and four in a ventral tray), one defensive 13mm (0.51in) MG 131 machine gun rear cockpit

Junkers Ju 88R-2

Equipped with FuG 220 radar, this Ju 88R-2 was operated by 8./Nachtjagdgeschwader 2 in 1944.

was equipped with Lichtenstein BC (FuG 202) radar. Eventually over 3200 C-series aircraft were completed, most of them being employed in the night fighter role.

The Ju 88R-1 and Ju 88R-2, with out-of-sequence designations, were developed once the BMW 801MA powerplant became available. This was the result of lessons learned with the C-series night fighters, which had

Junkers Ju 88G-1

This Ju 88G-1 carries FuG 220 equipment and was operated by 9./Nachtjagdgeschwader 3 at Lübeck-Blankensee in spring 1945.

Junkers Ju 88R-2

Weight (Maximum take-off) 12,105kg (26,686lb)
Dimensions Length: 14.4m (47ft 2in), Wingspan: 20m (65ft 7in), Height: 5m (16ft 7in)
Powerplant Two 1267kW (1700hp) BMW 801D piston radial engines
Speed 580km/h (360mph)
Range 1789km (1112 miles)
Ceiling 8200m (26,900ft)
Crew 3
Armament One 20mm (0.8in) MG FF cannon and three 7.92mm (0.31in) MG 17 machine guns (nose), two MG FF cannon (ventral gondola), one rear-firing 13mm (0.51in) MG 131 machine gun

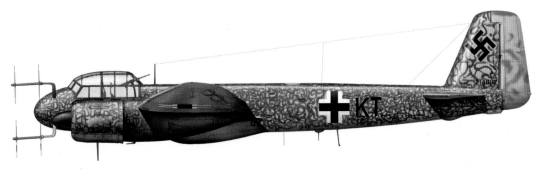

continued to add armour and high-drag antennas with a corresponding detrimental effect on performance. As the Ju 88R-1, the first of the re-engined R-series appeared soon after the Ju 88C-6b and combined the airframe of this type with the alternative engines. One example of the Ju 88R-1 (complete with Lichtenstein BC) fell into Allied hands when it was flown by its 10./ Nachtjagdgeschwader 3 crew to Dyce in Scotland on 9 May 1943, providing a technological windfall. The Ju 88R-2, meanwhile, was similar to the R-1 but featured BMW 801D engines.

Another night fighter subvariant of the Jumo-engined Ju 88C-6 was the Ju 88C-6c that was introduced in late 1943. This was equipped with improved Lichtenstein SN-2 (FuG 220) radar that was able to defeat the Window countermeasures dropped by RAF bombers.

Ju 88G

The definitive Ju 88 night fighter series was the Ju 88G, which began to replace the previous Ju 88C and Ju 88R versions in Luftwaffe service from early summer 1944. These were among the finest night fighters of the war, offering a combination of devastating firepower and increasingly effective airborne interception radar.

The initial prototype for the Ju 88G was the Ju 88 V58, based on a modified, BMW 801-powered Ju 88R-1. This featured an armament of six 20mm (0.8in) MG 151/20 cannon (two in the nose and four in a ventral tray) and also added the larger, angular tail fin of the Ju 188. A single 13mm (0.51in) MG 131 machine gun was provided for rear defence. This entered series production as the Ju 88G-1, in which the two nose cannon were deleted (they had been found to blind the pilot when fired at night).

The Ju 88G-1 was equipped from the start with Lichtenstein SN-2 radar and was also outfitted with Flensburg (FuG 227) gear, which included a wing-mounted antenna array that homed in on the Monica tail-warning radar carried by RAF bombers.

Captivity set-back

The first of the Ju 88G-1s entered service in early 1944 but the Luftwaffe was struck a significant blow when, on 13 July that year, an example of the aircraft landed by mistake at Woodbridge in Suffolk. The British

Junkers Ju 88G-6

Another aircraft equipped with FuG 220, this Ju 88G-6 saw service with II./Nachtjagdgeschwader 2 in early 1945, when it was captured by Allied forces at Fritzlar.

Junkers Ju 88G-6

Weight (Maximum take-off) 12,292kg (28,000lb)
Dimensions Length: 15.50m (50ft 9in), Wingspan: 20.08m (65ft 9in), Height: 5.07m (16ft 7in)
Powerplant Two 1286kW (1725hp) Junkers Jumo 213A V-12 piston radial engines
Speed 540km/h (335mph)
Range 2800km (1739 miles)
Ceiling 9400m (30,840ft)
Crew 4
Armament Six 20mm (0.8in) MG 151/20 cannon (two in the nose and four in a ventral tray), one rear-firing 13mm (0.51in) MG 131 machine gun

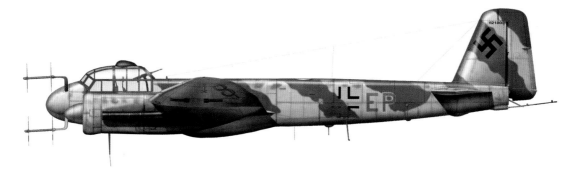

military were able to develop a successful jamming countermeasure to the Lichtenstein SN-2, while also being provided information on the Flensburg equipment.

By September 1944, the Ju 88G-1 and equally formidable Messerschmitt Bf 110G-4 were part of an inventory of 1018 Luftwaffe night fighters on strength, most of these being assigned to the Luftflotte Reich's I Jagdkorps. While previous Ju 88 night fighters had carried a standard crew of three, this was increased by the introduction of a second observer in the G series.

Subvariants

Key subvariants of the Ju 88G family were the Ju 88G-4 that incorporated various improvements that had been made since the Ju 88G-1 began to be fielded, and the Ju 88G-6a that was powered by a pair of BMW 801G engines. The G-series night fighters often were fitted with upward-firing 20mm (0.8in) MG 151/20 cannon in a *Schräge Musik* installation and sometimes also incorporated a rear-facing Lichtenstein SN-2 radar to provide tail warning.

The Ju 88G-6b designation covered aircraft that were provided with Naxos X (FuG 350) homing antennas. The Naxos gear, which worked by homing in on emissions from RAF bombers' H2S

Junkers Ju 88G-6b

This aircraft flew with Nachtjagdgeschwader 101 (NJG 101) from Ingolstadt, late 1944. Note the replacement rudder and the *Schräge Musik* oblique gun installation.

radars, was identified by a prominent bulge above the cockpit.

The next major improvement came with the Ju 88G-6c subvariant that was powered by two Jumo 213A engines. Externally, this aircraft could be differentiated by a forward row of cooling gills on the cowling and flame-dampers covering the exhausts stubs. The upward-firing cannon were moved forward and the internal fuel capacity was reduced accordingly to maintain the centre of gravity.

Only a small number of the Ju 88G-7 variant were produced, these entering service from late 1944. These were powered by a pair of Jumo 213E engines with MW50 water-methanol boosting. Their fuel capacity was slightly increased, and they also had the ability to carry a single drop tank.

Radar options

Subvariants of the Ju 88G-7 were characterized by their different avionics fits: the Ju 88G-7a was fitted with the Lichtenstein SN-2 (FuG 220) radar, while the Ju 88G-7b began life with the Lichtenstein SN-3 (FuG

Junkers Ju 88G-6b

Weight (Maximum take-off) 12,292kg (28,000lb)

Dimensions Length: 15.50m (50ft 9in), Wingspan: 20.08m (65ft 9in), Height: 5.07m (16ft 7in)

Powerplant Two 1250kW (1677hp) BMW 801G piston radial engines

Speed 540km/h (335mph)

Range 2200km (1367 miles)

Ceiling 9400m (30,840ft)

Crew 4

Armament Six 20mm (0.8in) MG 151/20 cannon (two in the nose and four in a ventral tray), one defensive 13mm (0.51in) MG 131 machine gun rear cockpit; one upward-firing MG 151/20 cannon in a *Schräge Musik* installation

Junkers Ju 88G-7a

This aircraft flew with Nachtjagdgeschwader 6 (NJG 6), from Schwäbisch Hall during the winter of 1944–45. Note that the tail has been painted to resemble a Ju 88C.

228) radar; but once this began to be subjected to jamming by the Allies it was superseded by the Neptun VR (FuG 218). The Neptun VR equipment featured a *Morgenstern* (morning star) antenna, often partially enclosed in a wooden nosecone.

Beginning with the Ju 88G-7a, variants of the night fighter began to feature refined 'stag's antlers' radar antennas on the nose, these now being canted to reduce the effects of interference. The final night fighter version in this prolific family was the Ju 88G-7c, which featured Berlin N-1a (FuG 340) in a reprofiled nose cone, but only around 10 examples made it as far as frontline units.

Proving highly resistant to the effect of Window, the Berlin N-1a was the Luftwaffe's first airborne radar to feature a dish antenna, inspired by the RAF's H2S kit, examples of which had been captured in December 1942.

The well-equipped Ju 88G night fighters were often used in the fighter-controller role, exploiting their comprehensive mission avionics to help guide less well-equipped Bf 109s

and Bf 110s towards their target. As the wartime situation became more desperate for Germany, examples were also pressed into use in a daytime role, primarily in an effort to blunt the advances of the Red Army from the east.

Close-support role

Other examples of the Ju 88G night fighter were used in the close support role during the offensive in the Ardennes in late 1944. By the time the war had ended, around 800 G-series aircraft had been completed.

In this later variant G-7a the antennas of the FuG 220 were canted to reduce interference.

Junkers Ju 88G-7a

Weight (Maximum take-off) 13,109kg (28,900lb)
Dimensions Length: 14.5m (47ft 6in), Wingspan: 22m (72ft 2in), Height: 5.07m (16ft 7in)
Powerplant Two 1287kW (1726hp) Jumo 213E engines with MW50 water-methanol boosting
Speed 647km/h (402mph)
Range 2200km (1367 miles)
Ceiling 9800m (32,100ft)
Crew 4
Armament Six 20mm (0.8in) MG 151/20 cannon (two in the nose and four in a ventral tray), one defensive 13mm (0.51in) MG 131 machine gun rear cockpit

Focke-Wulf Ta 154

The Ta 154 represented an attempt to provide the Luftwaffe with a high-performance night fighter that would nonetheless be manufactured using non-strategic materials – mainly wood.

Focke-Wulf Ta 154 V7

Focke-Wulf Ta 154 V7 TE+FK underwent tests at Lagenhagen, Germany, in spring 1944. This seventh prototype was painted in the RLM 75/76 camouflage pattern. Its fate is unknown.

The requirement for the aircraft emerged to counter the increasing ferocity of the Royal Air Force's night bombing campaign over Germany, targeting urban and industrial centres. In response, the *Reichsluftfahrtministerium* (German Air Ministry) ordered the development of a two-seat night fighter and issued a specification in August 1942.

Shoulder-wing monoplane

Facing competition from the Heinkel He 219, the Kurt Tank-designed Ta 154 was a twin-engine shoulder-wing monoplane of wooden construction throughout; as well as reducing the demands on scarce strategic materials, this was intended to ensure it could be manufactured by trained woodworkers. The powerplant consisted of a pair of 1119kW (1500hp) Jumo 211N 12-cylinder inverted-Vee engines.

The first prototype, the Ta 154 V1, took to the air at Hanover/ Langenhagen on 1 July 1943, with Tank himself at the controls. It was joined in the flight-test programme by the second prototype, the Ta 154 V2, which shared the same powerplant. The two aircraft were used for performance and handling trials before being joined by the third prototype, the Ta 154 V3, which introduced 1119kW (1500hp) Jumo 211R engines and completed a maiden flight on 25 November 1943. The Ta 154 V3 was also the first to feature mission equipment, in the form of a Lichtenstein BC-1 (FuG 202) radar.

The pre-production series of Ta 154A-0 aircraft were outfitted with armament, comprising single examples of the 20mm (0.8in) MG 151/20 and 30mm (1.18in) MK 108 cannon arranged to fire forward from positions on each side of the fuselage, below the cockpit.

Another four prototypes were completed and flown at Langenhagen between January and March 1944

Focke-Wulf Ta 154A-0

Weight (Maximum take-off) 9550kg (21,054lb)

Dimensions Length: 12.45m (40ft 10in), Wingspan: 16m (52ft 6in), Height: 3.5m (11ft 6in)

Powerplant Two 1119kW (1500hp) Junkers Jumo 211R V-12 liquid-cooled piston engines

Speed 644km/h (400mph)

Range 1365km (848 miles)

Ceiling 10,900m (35,800ft)

Crew 2

Armament One 20mm (0.8in) MG 151/20 and one 30mm (1.18in) MK 108 cannon

and a further eight examples of the Ta 154A-0 were completed at Erfurt, to acheive the original German Air Ministry development order.

Series production aircraft

Ten examples of the series-production Ta 154A-1 were built, these adding a single MK 108 cannon in a rear-fuselage installation, angled at 45 degrees and firing upwards and forwards.

With radar and armament, the aircraft boasted a top speed of over 644km/h (400mph), but the structural failure of two early production aircraft on 28 and 30 June 1944 led to the termination of the programme later that year. The reason for the losses was a failure of the adhesive that was used to bond the plywood used in the type's construction. While the prototypes and pre-production aircraft had used Tego-Film adhesive, this was replaced by an inferior type after the responsible factory at Wuppertal was bombed.

Mistel composites

As well as around 50 Ta 154A-1 production aircraft, six examples were completed as Ta 154A-2/U3 aircraft for use in *Mistel* composite aircraft. These were based on converted Ta 154A-0 pre-production aircraft with the addition of a 2000kg (4409lb) warhead in the nose and supports for the Fw 190 upper component, whose pilot controlled the combination.

The Ta 154A-3 was a proposed two-seat conversion trainer, while the production Ta 154A-4 saw limited service with 1./Nachtjagdgeschwader 3 and Nachtschlachtgruppe 10. Some of the Junkers Jumo 211N-powered Ta 154A-4s were also fitted with FuG 218 Neptun radar.

The Focke-Wulf Ta 154 V1 prototype (TE+FE) undergoing trials, July 1943.

Heinkel He 219 *Uhu*

The He 219 *Uhu* ('eagle owl') had the potential to be one of the most capable night fighters in service with the Luftwaffe.

It emerged from a private-venture study, the Heinkel P.1060 fighter-bomber, which began to be the subject of official interest in 1941, when there was a view to developing it for the night fighter role. The resulting He 219 was an all-metal shoulder-wing monoplane, with accommodation for a pilot and navigator, seated back to back. The aircraft was schemed with ejection seats – being the first operational aircraft to feature these – and it was also the Luftwaffe's first operational aircraft with tricycle landing gear.

An initial prototype completed a maiden flight on 15 November 1942, under the power of a pair of Daimler-Benz DB 603A engines each rated at 1305kW (1750hp). A second prototype took to the air in December, featuring a revised armament configuration. After evaluation of one of the protypes in simulated combat with a Dornier Do 217N and a Junkers Ju 88S, an order for 100 aircraft was increased to 300. In the meantime, further prototypes joined the evaluation programme.

First production aircraft

The first pre-production He 219A-0 aircraft began to be issued to 1./Nachtjagdgeschwader 1 at Venlo in the Netherlands and, on the night of 11 June 1943, pilot Werner Streib succeeded in shooting down five Royal Air Force Lancaster bombers in a single sortie. The first six operational

This post-war view of an He 219 shows the stalky nosewheel, which turned through 90 degrees and retracted to lie flat beneath the cockpit.

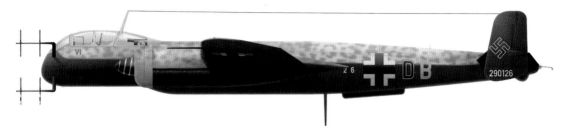

Heinkel He 219A-2 Uhu

He 219A-2 D5+BL of Nachtjagdgeschwader 3 was captured at Gove, Denmark, in May 1945.

sorties flown by the unit with the *Uhu* resulted in claims of 20 RAF aircraft destroyed, including six of the highly-valued Mosquitoes.

He 219A-0 aircraft were produced in He 219A-0/R1 and R2 subtypes, with belly trays housing either four 30mm (1.18in) MK 108 cannon or four 30mm MK 103 cannon, respectively.

Heinkel He 219A-7 Uhu

Weight (Maximum take-off) 15,300 (33,730lb)

Dimensions Length: 15.55m (50ft 11in), Wingspan: 18.5m (60ft 8in), Height: 4.1m (13ft 5in)

Powerplant Two 1417kW (1900hp) Daimler-Benz DB 603G engines

Speed 670km/h (420mph)

Range 1540km (957 miles)

Ceiling 12,700m (41,666ft)

Crew 2

Armament Two 20mm (0.8in) MG 151/20s (wing roots), plus two MG 151/20s and two 30mm (1.18in) MK 103 cannon (ventral tray)

Series production night fighter

The He 219A-1 was to have been a reconnaissance bomber but work on this was abandoned in favour of the He 219A-2 that was the initial series-production night fighter. In its He 219A-2/R1 form it was armed with two MK 108 or MK 103 cannon and two 20mm (0.8in) MG 151/20 cannon in a ventral tray, plus a pair of MG 151/20s in the wing roots – the latter were a standard option in all He 219 night fighters. Aircraft were also retroactively equipped with a pair of MK 108 cannon firing obliquely upward and forward in a *Schräge Musik* installation behind the cockpit.

The He 219A-2/R1 was initially equipped with Lichtenstein C-1 (FuG 212) radar with four small antenna arrays on the nose; subsequent He 219A-2s carried a single antenna for the C-1 and four large 'stag's antlers'

Heinkel He 219A-2 Uhu

Weight (Maximum take-off) 15,300 (33,730lb)

Dimensions Length: 15.55m (50ft 11in), Wingspan: 18.5m (60ft 8in), Height: 4.1m (13ft 5in)

Powerplant Two 1305kW (1750hp) Daimler-Benz DB 603A engines

Speed 665km/h (413mph)

Range 1540km (957 miles)

Ceiling 12,700m (41,666ft)

Crew 2

Armament Two 30mm (1.18in) MK 108 or MK 103 cannon and two 20mm (0.8in) MG 151/20 cannon (ventral tray), plus two MG 151/20s (wing roots)

Heinkel He 219A-7 Uhu

Another of the Nachtjagdgeschwader 3 aircraft captured at Gove, Denmark, in May 1945, D5+CL was an example of the He 219A-7 variant.

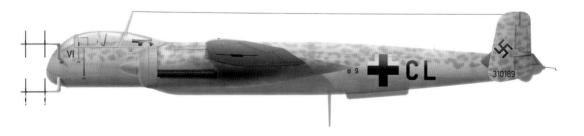

antennas for the new Lichtenstein SN-2 (FuG 220).

He 219A-5, A-6 and A-7

The next version to see quantity production was the He 219A-5, which was generally similar to the He 219A-2. In its He 219A-5/R1 form this was powered by a pair of 1342kW (1800hp) DB 603A engines and featured increased fuel capacity. The He 219A-5/R4 differed In carrying a third crew member and had a stepped cockpit with the pivoted 13mm (0.51in) machine gun reinstated; it was also armed with two MK 108s in the ventral tray. Some of the A-5s were not fitted with the Lichtenstein C-1 radar and instead often had a slanted arrangement of Lichtenstein SN-2 antennas to reduce interference.

Streamlined version

In order to have a better chance of catching the RAF's Mosquito, the He 219A-6 was created as a stripped-down version, based on the He 219A-2/R1 but powered by 1305kW (1750hp) DB 603L engines and armed with four MG 151/20 cannon.

The He 219A-7 was similar to the He 219A-5 but introduced improved supercharger intakes for its DB 603G engines, which were each rated at 1417kW (1900hp). While it carried the now-standard *Schräge Musik*

installation, the He 219A-7/R1 also had two MG 151/20s in the wing roots, plus two MG 151/20s and two MK 103s in the ventral tray.

The He 219A-7/R2 again differed in its armament, with two MK 108s and two MK 103s in the ventral tray, while the He 219A-7/R3 had a ventral tray accommodating two MK 108s and two MG 151/20s. The He 219A-7/R4 introduced tail-warning radar but reduced the ventral tray complement to just two MG 151/20s.

Only six of the He 219A-7/R5 subvariant were built and these were essentially similar to the He 219A-7/R3 but with a pair of 1417kW (1900hp) Junkers Jumo 213E engines and a water-methanol injection system. Finally, a pair of 1864kW (2500hp) Jumo 222A/B engines differentiated the He 219A-7/R6, only a single example of which was ever completed. In terms of radar, the A-7 added the newer Neptune (FuG 218) to the Lichtenstein SN-2.

He 219B-1

Limited efforts were made on the He 219B series, which yielded a single He 219B-1 with DB 603Aa engines and a three-man crew, although Jumo 222A/B engines had initially been planned. Meanwhile, the He 219B-2 was similar to the He 219A-6, but with only two MG 151/20 cannon.

Despite its promise, the He 219 proved to be a victim of official disinterest and the programme was cancelled in May 1944. Nevertheless, production deliveries were made, and the aircraft also saw operational service with Nachtjagdgruppe 10.

Heinkel He 219B Uhu

Weight (Maximum take-off) 15,300 (33,730lb)

Dimensions Length: 15.55m (50ft 11in), Wingspan: 18.5m (60ft 8in), Height: 4.1m (13ft 5in)

Powerplant Two 1305kW (1750hp) Daimler-Benz DB 603Aa engines

Speed 670km/h (420mph)

Range 1540km (957 miles)

Ceiling 12,700m (41,666ft)

Crew 3

Armament Two 20mm (0.8in) MG 151/20s and two 30mm (1.18in) MK 103s cannon (ventral tray)

Heinkel He 219B Uhu

An artist's interpretation of the He 219B *Uhu* with Jumo 222 engine and extended wingspan. Note the large ducted spinner and numerous exhaust pipes to accommodate the engine's 24 cylinders.

Arado Ar 240

Design of the Ar 240 was based around the FA-13 armament system comprising guns in remotely controlled barbettes, aimed with periscopic sights.

Development of the FA-13 was undertaken by a team consisting of Arado, Rheinmetall-Borsig and the Deutsche Versuchsanstalt für Luftfahrt (German Laboratory for Aviation) and the barbettes were initially tested in a Messerschmitt Bf 110.

Remote-controlled armaments

In 1938 the *Reichsluftfahrtministerium* (German Air Ministry) requested proposals for a twin-engine aircraft able to carry two examples of the FA-13. Arado's E.240, designed by Hans Rebeski, faced competition from the AGO Ao 225. The former was awarded a contract, as the Ar 240, but the initial two prototypes were not yet fitted with the FA-13, which was suffering teething troubles. The initial prototype of the mid-wing monoplane was powered by two 802kW (1075hp) Daimler-Benz DB 601A engines. The second aircraft introduced armament, albeit not the FA-13 – instead it was fitted with two forward-firing 20mm (0.8in) MG 151/20 cannon in the nose and two 7.92mm (0.31in) MG 17 machine guns in the wing roots.

Arado Ar 240A-02

Both the Arado Ar 240A-01 and -02 were issued to Jagdgeschwader (JG) 5 and based in Petsamo in northern Finland, where they were used for reconnaissance missions.

The initial two prototypes revealed some stability problems, addressed in the third aircraft that featured a fuselage 'stretch' of 1.25m (4ft 1.5in). The pressurised cockpit was also moved forward and the aircraft featured a new tail cone, with small fins, instead of the previous tail-mounted dive-brake. The third aircraft, which took to the air in spring 1941, was also the first with the FA-13 system – barbettes were fitted above and below the fuselage, behind the cockpit. Each was armed with a pair of 7.92mm (0.31in) MG 81 machine guns. However, in summer 1941 the barbettes were removed and replaced with cameras for operational evaluation with the 3./Aufklärungsgruppe Oberbefehlshaber der Luftwaffe. The fourth prototype was powered by a pair of 1305kW (1750hp) DB 603A engines.

Arado Ar 240A-02

Weight (Maximum take-off) 9540kg (20,790lb)
Dimensions Length: 12.80m (42ft), Wingspan: 13.33m (43ft 9in), Height: 3.95m (12ft 11in)
Powerplant Two 877kW (1176hp) Daimler-Benz DB 601E 12 cylinder in-line piston engines
Speed 620km/h (384mph)
Range 2000km (1240 miles)
Ceiling 10,500m (34,400ft)
Crew 2
Armament Two fixed forward-firing 7.92mm (0.31in) MG 17 machine guns and four 7.92mm (0.31in) machine guns in remotely-controlled barbettes

Five pre-production Ar 240A-0 aircraft were completed, the first two as armed reconnaissance aircraft, appearing in October 1942; the third with a pair of 1402kW (1880hp) BMW 801TJ radial engines; the last two, both unarmed, were powered by DB 603A engines.

Maiden flight

Two pre-production Ar 240B aircraft were flown in October and December 1942, powered by 1100kW (1475hp) DB 605A engines with water-methanol fuel injection. These were followed by the Ar 240C, which featured a new wing of increased span and refined profile.

Four pre-production C-series aircraft were completed as heavy fighter-bombers and flown in 1943, with 1305kW (1750hp) DB 603A-

2 powerplants. The last two had a power-boost system with nitrous oxide injection. The first C-series machines were armed with four forward-firing 20mm (0.8in) MG 131/20 cannon and two barbettes, each fitted with two 13mm (0.51in) MG 131 machine guns. The second aircraft added another two forward-firing MG 151/20s in a ventral housing and was intended as a night fighter.

The C-series was planned for production as the Ar 240C-1 heavy fighter, C-2 night fighter, C-3 light bomber and C-4 high-altitude reconnaissance aircraft, all with 1417kW (1900hp) DB 603G engines. Although AGO received a production contract for 40 Ar 240s, in December 1942, the programme was cancelled as a result of continued problems with the aircraft.

Arado Ar 240C-2

This Ar 240C night fighter, BO+RD, was apparently used for defence of the Arado plant in Brandenburg-Neuendorf, Germany, in 1943.

Arado Ar 240C-2

Weight (Maximum take-off) 9540kg (20,790lb)
Dimensions Length: 12.80m (42ft), Wingspan: 13.33m (43ft 9in), Height: 3.95m (12ft 11in)
Powerplant Two 1417kW (1900hp) Daimler-Benz DB 603G 12 cylinder in-line piston engines
Speed 620km/h (384mph)
Range 2000km (1240 miles)
Ceiling 10,500m (34,400ft)
Crew 2
Armament Four fixed forward-firing 20mm (0.8in) MG 131/20 cannon and four 13mm (0.51in) MG 131 machine guns in remotely-controlled barbettes

---

Arado Ar 240 V2 (KK+CD), the second prototype to be produced, first flew on 6 April 1941. Thereafter it was used in an experimental role.

Messerschmitt Me 210

The early success of the Bf 110 twin-engine heavy fighter in Luftwaffe hands encouraged Messerschmitt to pursue development of a follow-on *Zerstörer*, the Me 210, which was planned to be powered by a pair of 783kW (1050hp) Daimler-Benz DB 601A engines.

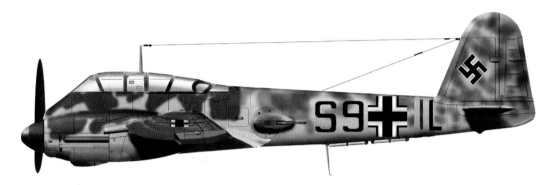

A pre-series Me 210A-0 of 3./
Schnellkampfgeschwader 210, circa 1942.
This aircraft belly-landed at Tours, France, on
9 January 1942, after an engine failure. The
crew were *Leutnant* Gerhard Schwab and radio
operator *Unteroffizier* Karl-Fritz Schröder.

Messerschmitt Me 210A-0

Weight (Maximum take-off) 9705kg (21,396lb)
Dimensions Length: 12.2m (40ft), Wingspan:
16.3m (53ft 6in), Height: 4.2m (13ft 9in)
Powerplant Two 783kW (1050hp) Daimler-Benz
DB 601A engines
Speed 463km/h (288mph)
Range 1818km (1130 miles)
Ceiling 8,900m (29,200ft)
Crew 2
Armament Two 20mm (0.8in) MG 151/20 cannon,
two 7.92mm (0.3in) MG 17 machine guns, two
remotely-controlled rear-firing 13mm (0.51in) MG
131 machine guns

A corresponding requirement for a replacement for the Bf 110 was issued by the *Reichsluftfahrtministerium* (German Air Ministry) as early as 1938; this called for an aircraft that would offer the required flexibility to undertake air combat, ground attack, dive-bombing and reconnaissance roles. In the summer of that year the company was awarded a contract for its Me 210 design, while examples of the Ar 240 were requested from Arado as a potential backup. Such was the confidence of the Air Ministry that Messerschmitt was authorised, at this early stage, to produce long-lead items – including wing spars – for the envisaged quantity production that would follow.

In terms of design, the Me 210 shared much commonality with the Bf 110, but introduced some novelties, especially with the armament. The new heavy fighter introduced remotely-controlled rear-firing weapons in the form of a 13mm (0.51in) MG 131 machine gun installed in an electrically powered barbette on each side of the rear fuselage. These barbettes were

mounted on a rotating drum, and each could traverse through 90 degrees. They were aimed by the observer, seated in the rear of the bulged glazed canopy, facing aft.

Other internal armament comprised a pair of 20mm (0.8in) MG 151/20 cannon and two 7.92mm (0.3in) MG 17 machine guns mounted beneath the cockpit floor, flanking a small bomb bay. A nose that was much shortened in comparison to that of the Bf 110 ensured the pilot enjoyed excellent visibility in the forward aspect.

First prototype

A first prototype, the Me 210 V1, took to the air on 5 September 1939 with Hermann Wurster at the controls, but immediately demonstrated handling difficulties in terms of yaw and pitch and extreme instability. Despite repeated modifications, including the addition of a single large fin, the Me 210's propensity to stall and spin was never fully addressed. Nonetheless, it was ordered into production for the Luftwaffe; by 1941 there were both pre-production Me 210A-0 and initial

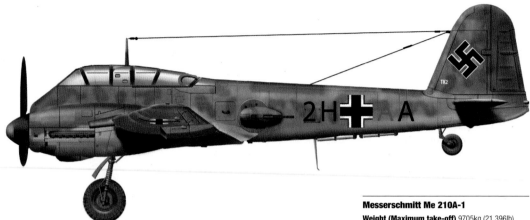

Messerschmitt Me 210A-1

Me 210A-1 2H+AA of Erprobungstaffel 210 was
based at Soesterberg, Netherlands.

The Me 210 was plagued with vicious and
unpredictable handling qualities. The aircraft
shown in this photograph was fitted with the
longer fuselage, which largely cured the design's
major faults.

series-production Me 210A-1 aircraft
emerging from the production lines.

Production versions of the
Me 210 were schemed as the Me
210A-1 bomber/bomber-destroyer
and the Me 210A-2 dive-bomber/
bomber-destroyer. In order to operate
in the dive-bomber role, the aircraft
was originally designed with 'Venetian
blind' dive brakes mounted in the
wings.

Messerschmitt Me 210A-1

Weight (Maximum take-off) 9705kg (21,396lb)

Dimensions Length: 12.2m (40ft), Wingspan:
16.3m (53ft 6in), Height: 4.2m (13ft 9in)

Powerplant Two 990kW (1330hp) Daimler-Benz
DB 601F engines

Speed 463km/h (288mph)

Range 1818km (1130 miles)

Ceiling 8900m (29,200ft)

Crew 2

Armament Two 20mm (0.8in) MG 151/20 cannon,
two 7.92mm (0.3in) MG 17 machine guns, two
remotely-controlled rear-firing 13mm (0.51in) MG
131 machine guns

However, after around 200 examples of the Me 210 had been completed, further manufacture was axed in April 1942 and instead the Bf 110 was reinstated to production. Work to refine the basic design of the Me 210 continued, however, now focusing on the improved Me 410. In the meantime, however, a modified Me 210A-0 had been flown with a new, longer and deeper rear fuselage, slatted outer wings and other changes. This demonstrated much improved handling and existing aircraft were modified to the same standard, entering service with 16./Kampfgeschwader 6 and III./Zerstörergeschwader 1, both of which served in the Mediterranean theatre.

A small number of aircraft were also completed as Me 210B reconnaissance derivatives, while others were outfitted as dual-control trainers. Ultimately, the aircraft was destined to enjoy only a brief frontline career with the Luftwaffe, before the improved Me 410 became available in numbers.

Hungarian production
Production of the Me 210 was also undertaken in Hungary, by the Danube Aircraft Factory, using jigs and tooling that had been provided by Messerschmitt. The Hungarian-built machines were designated Me 210C-1

and Me 210Ca-1 and featured slats on the leading edges of the wing as well as the redesigned rear fuselage of the subsequent Me 410.

The C-series aircraft were powered by a pair of 1100kW (1475hp) Daimler-Benz DB 605B engines produced under licence by Manfred Weiss. Total production of the Me 210C amounted to 267 aircraft, a third of which were delivered to the Hungarian Air Force, while the remainder were provided to the Luftwaffe. Thereafter, the Danube works switched to production of the single-engine Bf 109G.

Refining failed design
The Me 210's failure had a significant knock-on effect for the fortunes of the German company, and led to the resignation of its chief designer, Willy Messerschmitt. Despite this, the firm continued to refine the basic design of the Me 210 and it was thoroughly reworked as the Me 410. While this carried a different designation to signal its break from the past, the initial Me 410 prototype was an adapted Me 210A-0 pre-production aircraft and shared many similarities.

Messerschmitt Me 210Ca-1
This Hungarian Air Force Me 210Ca-1 served with 102/1.Század 'Tigris' in 1944.

Messerschmitt Me 210Ca-1
Weight (Maximum take-off) 9705kg (21,396lb)
Dimensions Length: 12.2m (40ft), Wingspan: 16.3m (53ft 6in), Height: 4.2m (13ft 9in)
Powerplant Two 1100kW (1475hp) Daimler-Benz DB 605B engines
Speed 463km/h (288mph)
Range 1818km (1130 miles)
Ceiling 8900m (29,200ft)
Crew 2
Armament Two 20mm (0.8in) MG 151/20 cannon, two 7.92mm (0.3in) MG 17 machine guns, two remotely-controlled rear-firing 13mm (0.51in) MG 131 machine guns; maximum 1000kg (2204lb) internal bombload

---

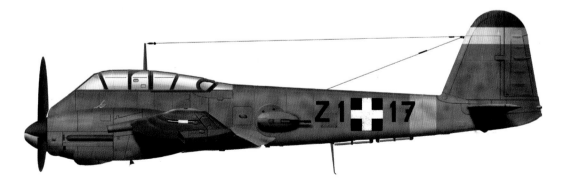

Messerschmitt Me 410

The Me 410 *Hornisse* ('hornet') was a thoroughly improved development of the Me 210, featuring a lengthened rear fuselage of new design and a wing fitted with automatic leading-edge slats.

The wing also now featured a straight taper, rather than the five degree leading-edge sweepback of the Me 210. The revised powerplant was provided by a pair of 1305kW (1750hp) Daimler-Benz DB 603A engines.

A prototype for the Me 410 was constructed on the basis of an Me 210A-0 pre-production aircraft and several other Me 210s were completed to a similar standard for test and evaluation. Initial trials in autumn 1942 yielded positive results and full-scale production was therefore authorized to begin in January 1943.

Me 410A series

The initial-production Me 410A series included the Me 410A-1 high-speed bomber (*Schnellbomber*) and the Me 410A-2 heavy fighter/bomber-destroyer (*Zerstörer*), while the Me 410A-3 was a reconnaissance variant. The first deliveries of the A-series to the Luftwaffe were made in January 1943 and a total of 48 had been handed over by April that year. These early deliveries were used to replace examples of the Dornier Do 217 and Junkers Ju 88.

The demand for additional aircraft saw the Messerschmitt plant at Augsburg turn out 457 aircraft by the end of 1943 and, in order to further expand the production effort, Dornier also started to manufacture the *Hornisse* from early 1944.

Further development of the basic design led to the subsequent B-series, another series-production version, now with a pair of 1417kW (1900hp) DB 603G engines. Derivatives included

This Me 410A-3 from 2. Staffel/Aufklärungsgruppe 122 was captured by US forces in Sardinia.

Messerschmitt Me 410A-1/U3

'Yellow 7' was a Me 410A-1/U3 sub-variant operated by II./Zerstörergeschwader 26 based at Hildesheim, Germany, in February 1944. It was a single-seat conversion designed to assess the GM-1 nitrous oxide power-boost system. The lateral gun barbettes were also deleted.

Messerschmitt Me 410A-3

Weight (Maximum take-off) 9651kg (21,276lb)
Dimensions Length: 12.4m (40ft 11.5in), Wingspan: 16.3m (53ft 7.7in), Height: 4.3m (14ft)
Powerplant One Two 1300kW (1750hp) Daimler-Benz DB 603A V-12 inverted-V piston engines
Speed 624km/h (388mph)
Range 1200km (746 miles)
Ceiling 10,000m (33,000ft)
Crew 2
Armament Two 20mm (0.8in) MG 151/20 cannon, two 7.92mm (0.31in) MG 17 machine guns, two remotely-controlled rear-firing 13mm (0.51in) MG 131 machine guns

the Me 410B-1, Me 410B-2 and Me 410B-3, which were equivalent to the previous Me 410A-1, Me 410A-2 and Me 410A-3. The next subvariants were the Me 410B-5 anti-shipping/torpedo-bomber that was undergoing tests as the war came to an end. The Me 410B-5 was intended to employ the Friedensengel gliding torpedo, SB 800RS Kurt anti-ship rolling bomb and the SB 1000/410 blast weapon.

Another variant envisaged for anti-shipping operations was the Me 410B-6; both the Me 410B-5 and B-6 were fitted with the Hohentwiel (FuG 200) radar for their maritime duties. Typical armament for the anti-shipping Me 410B-6 comprised two 30mm (1.18in) MK 103 cannon and two 13mm (0.51in) MG 131 machine guns. There was also a day reconnaissance version, the Me 410B-7, while the

Messerschmitt Me 410A-1

Weight (Maximum take-off) 9651kg (21,276lb)
Dimensions Length: 12.4m (40ft 11.5in), Wingspan: 16.3m (53ft 7.7in), Height: 4.3m (14ft)
Powerplant One Two 1300kW (1750hp) Daimler-Benz DB 603A V-12 inverted-V piston engines
Speed 624km/h (388mph)
Range 1690km (1050 miles)
Ceiling 10,000m (33,000ft)
Crew 2
Armament Two 20mm (0.8in) MG 151/20 cannon, two 7.92mm (0.31in) MG 17 machine guns; maximum 1000kg (2204lb) internal bombload

Messerschmitt Me 410A-3/U1

Me 410A-3/U1 sub-variant F6+WK of II./Fernaufklärungsgruppe 122, captured by Allied forces in Sicily and shipped to the US for evaluation.

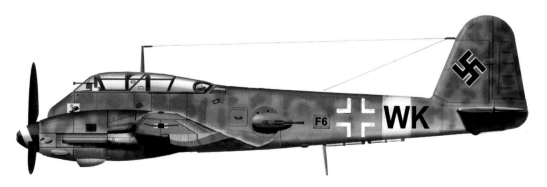

night-reconnaissance equivalent was the Me 410B-8. These two recce machines only advanced as far as the prototype stage. Various different armament 'kits' were also available for the Me 410B under the 'U' and 'R' suffixes, including the U1 that provided a camera in the rear fuselage for reconnaissance work.

Most others featured variations of cannon armament, including 30mm (1.18in) MK 103 or MK 108 weapons, up to six 20mm (0.8in) MG 151/20 cannon or (in the U4 sub-variant) a single 50mm (1.96in) BK 5 cannon. The Me 410B-2/U4, meanwhile, combined the BK 5 with a pair of MK 108s.

Both the Me 410A-3 and B-3 reconnaissance versions included a two-camera installation in a deepened weapons bay below the cockpit. They proved far more successful in service than the extemporised U1 adaptations and operated in all theatres with virtual impunity, with the exception of the United Kingdom.

Daytime defender

As the Allies increased the intensity of their daylight bombing activities over Germany, as of mid-1944 the Me 410 was increasingly being removed from a variety of other assignments In disparate theatres and pressed into use on daytime home defence duties.

Messerschmitt Me 410-B1/U4

Me 410B-1/U4 3U+CC was operated by Stab II./ Zerstörergeschwader 26 in 1944. The aircraft was stationed at Königsberg-Neumark, where it was captured complete and then evaluated by the RAF at Farnborough after the war.

In particular, the variants outfitted with heavy cannon were diverted to these duties, including the anti-shipping Me 410B-5 and B-6, which had their maritime radar removed.

Rocket armament

In one effort to improve the *Hornisse*'s chances of destroying bomber formations, tests were made of a rotary rocket launcher, based on the Werfergranate 21, a 210mm (8.75in) mortar that was used by Bf 109G day-fighters. The six-barrel launcher was installed in the Me 410's weapons bay, with the lower tube exposed and angled outwards. Once lined up on a bomber, the pilot could fire all six rockets within two seconds. Initial trials almost resulted in the loss of the launch aircraft and it seems unlikely that this system was ever used in operational service.

In its bomber-destroyer role, the Me 410 offered a useful turn of speed and impressive firepower and was successful in bringing down many US Army Air Force 'heavies'. On the

other hand, it was unable to hold its own when faced by more agile escort fighters, which were easily able to outmanoeuvre the German fighter.

Other examples of the *Hornisse* were engaged in fighter-bomber attacks against targets in southern England, operating by day and night. Despite these important missions, the Me 410 was judged to offer only a limited advantage over the well-established Bf 110 and, in September 1944, the decision was taken to terminate production in favour of the earlier design. By the time production came to an end, a total of 1160 Me 410s had been built.

Other versions

Cancelled versions all focused on improving high-altitude performance

Messerschmitt Me 410B-1/U4

Weight (Maximum take-off) 9651kg (21,276lb)

Dimensions Length: 12.4m (40ft 11.5in), Wingspan: 16.3m (53ft 7.7in), Height: 4.3m (14ft)

Powerplant Two 1417kW (1900hp) Daimler-Benz DB 603G engines

Speed 624km/h (388mph)

Range 1200km (746 miles)

Ceiling 10,000m (33,000ft)

Crew 2

Armament One 50mm (1.96in) BK 5 cannon; two remotely-controlled rear-firing 13mm (0.51in) MG 131 machine guns

An unusual feature of the Me 210/410 was the under-cockpit bomb bay. Bombs were loaded on the ground, and then winched into place.

Messerschmitt Me 410B-2/U2R2

Weight (Maximum take-off) 9651kg (21,276lb)
Dimensions Length: 12.4m (40ft 11.5in),
Wingspan: 16.3m (53ft 7.7in), Height: 4.3m (14ft)
Powerplant Two 1417kW (1900hp) Daimler-Benz
DB 603G engines
Speed 624km/h (388mph)
Range 1200km (746 miles)
Ceiling 10,000m (33,000ft)
Crew 2
Armament Two 20mm (0.8in) MG 151/20 cannon,
two 7.92mm (0.31in) MG 17 machine guns,
two 13mm (0.51in) MG 131 machine guns; two
remotely-controlled rear-firing 13mm (0.51in) MG
131 machine guns; maximum 1000kg (2204lb)
internal bombload

Messerschmitt Me 410B-2/U2R2

Me 410B-2/U2 9K+VV was assigned to 10./
Kampfgeschwader 51 in Germany – probably at
Munich-Riem – in early 1945.

for day/night fighter variants through the introduction of longer-span wings and more powerful engines. These included the Me 410C, which would have had much longer wings and more powerful turbochargers in annular cowlings. Powerplant options comprised the DB 603Z, Jumo 213E/JZ or BMW 801TJ. The Me 410C would also have incorporated a stretched fuselage and revised undercarriage with twin wheels on the main units; the revised cowlings and undercarriage were tested on modified Me 410A/Bs prior to cancellation of the C-series. Another proposed long-span development was the similar Me

410D, with DB 603Z engines and long-span wings. This was intended to have outer wing panels made of wood, as well as a revised nose section to provide an even better view for the pilot.

However, problems with the manufacture of the wooden wing panels forced its cancellation and a switch to the proposed Me 410H. This was to have been essentially similar to the Me 410B-2 but with extra un-tapered wing panels immediately outboard of the engines, for a new wingspan of around 23m (75ft); modifications of a first H-series aircraft began, but were never completed.

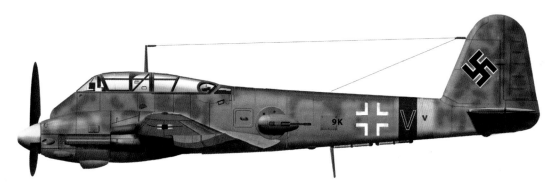

JET AND ROCKET FIGHTERS

Germany was the first country to fly an air-breathing jet, the Heinkel He 178, on 27 August 1939. The Luftwaffe made steady progress towards operational jet aircraft as other manufacturers were encouraged into the turbine propulsion field by the development of powerplants produced notably by Heinkel and Junkers. The Messerschmitt Me 262 achieved operational status in summer 1944. Meanwhile, work also focussed on rocket propulsion, leading to the Me 163, which proved to be the fastest combat aircraft produced during World War II.

This chapter includes the following aircraft:

- Messerschmitt Me 163 *Komet*
- Messerschmitt Me 262
- Heinkel He 162 *Volksjäger*
- Bachem Ba 349 *Natter*

A Messerschmitt Me 163 *Komet* is retreived and moved by Luftwaffe ground crew using a Scheuschlepper tractor and trailer after landing.

Messerschmitt Me 163 *Komet*

A unique rocket-powered fighter, the Me 163 *Komet* ('Comet') was derived from a long period of studies into tailless sailplane designs undertaken by Alexander Lippisch, beginning around 15 years before the outbreak of the war.

Messerschmitt Me 163B (V41)

Weight (Maximum take-off) 4310kg (9500lb)

Dimensions Length: 5.7m (18ft 8in), Wingspan: 9.3m (30ft 6in), Height: 2.76m (9ft)

Powerplant One Walter HWK 109-509A rocket motor delivering 14.71 kN (3307lb) of thrust

Speed 900km/h (560mph)

Range 35.5km (22 miles)

Ceiling 12,000m (39,370ft)

Crew 1

Armament Two 30mm (1.18in) MK 108 cannon

The aerodynamicist joined Messerschmitt, together with his design team, in January 1939 and then started work adapting the DFS 194 tailless research glider to accommodate a powerplant, in the form of the 3.92kN (882lb) thrust Walter rocket motor. After the aircraft was successfully tested – including demonstrating a speed of 550km/h (342mph) – Messerschmitt received an order for six prototypes of the combat-optimized Me 163A.

New speed

The initial prototype Me 163A V1 was completed as a glider and was carried aloft by a Bf 110. Beginning in late summer 1941, additional, powered prototypes began to be tested at the Peenemünde research facility, these now being fitted with the Walter HWK RII-203b rocket motor that developed 7.35kN (1635lb) of thrust and was powered by a combination of T-Stoff (hydrogen peroxide) and C-Stoff

(hydrazine hydrate, methyl alcohol and water) propellants.

Speeds of up to 885km/h (550mph) were recorded. On 2 October 1941, one of the Me 163As, piloted by Heini Dittmar, was towed aloft to an altitude of 4000m (13,125ft) before the engine was fired, after which it achieved a speed of 1003.9km/h (623.85mph), before the aircraft lost stability as a result of compressibility effects. Test pilot Dittmar managed to regain control of the aircraft and subsequently the design of the wing was altered to address the problem.

However, the Me 163 suffered further issues during its development, chief among which were those related to the highly unstable liquid fuel used by the rocket motor and the jettisonable wheeled dolly/retractable

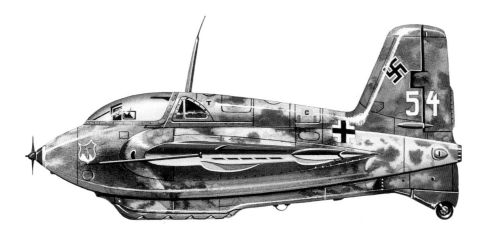

skid landing gear. After the six Me 163A prototypes, Messerschmitt completed a pre-production series of 10 Me 163A-0 aircraft, manufacture of which was subcontracted to Wolf Hirth. These were used as training gliders.

After a thorough redesign, orders were placed for six more prototypes and 70 production examples of the improved Me 163B series. These were now named *Komet* and intended to serve as point-defence interceptors. The pre-production prototypes were designated Me 163B-1a, and the first production deliveries of the Me 163B-1a followed in May 1944.

Launch procedure

The operating procedure involved launching under rocket power and immediately jettisoning the dolly undercarriage. The *Komet* then climbed on the power of its rocket motor at an angle of 45 degrees, heading toward the bomber formation. At around 9144m (30,000ft), the rocket fighter levelled out and dived to attack the bomber stream, typically flying at a height of 6096–7620m (20–25,000ft).

Messerschmitt Me 163B-1a Komet
'White 54' was a Me 163B-1a assigned to 14./ Jagdgeschwader 400 based at Brandis in Germany in late 1944 and early 1945. This *Staffel* served as the *Ergänzungsstaffel* (Operational Conversion Unit) for JG 400.

After the rocket engine cut out, the *Komet* would rely on its momentum to carry out repeated attacks on the bombers. Finally, after all effective speed and height had been lost, the *Komet* pilot would glide back to base where the aircraft would land on its retractable skid.

It was during this return-to-base phase that the Me 163 was most vulnerable to attack by Allied fighters. Data gathered after the war suggested that around 80 per cent of *Komet* losses occurred during take-off or landing, while another 15 per cent were due to loss of control in a compressibility dive or fire in the air. The remaining five per cent of losses were due to combat action.

The Me 163B-1 first went into action on a significant scale on 28 July 1944, when a group of six aircraft from 1./Jagdgeschwader 400 – the initial

Messerschmitt Me 163B-1a Komet
Weight (Maximum take-off) 4310kg (9500lb)
Dimensions Length: 5.85m (19ft 2in), Wingspan: 9.4m (30ft 7in), Height: 2.76m (9ft)
Powerplant One Walter HWK 109-509A rocket motor delivering 14.71 kN (3307lb) of thrust
Speed 955km/h (593mph)
Range 35.5km (22 miles)
Ceiling 12,000m (39,370ft)
Crew 1
Armament Two 30mm (1.18in) MK 108 cannon

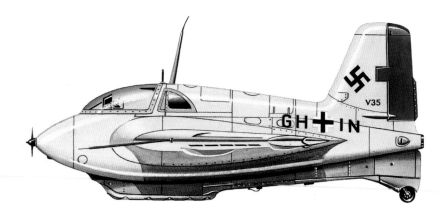

Messerschmitt Me 163B-1 Komet

Weight (Maximum take-off) 4310kg (9500lb)

Dimensions Length: 5.85m (19ft 2in), Wingspan: 9.4m (30ft 7in), Height: 2.76m (9ft)

Powerplant One Walter HWK 109-509A rocket motor delivering 14.71 kN (3307lb) of thrust

Speed 955km/h (593mph)

Range 35.5km (22 miles)

Ceiling 12,000m (39,370ft)

Crew 1

Armament Two 30mm (1.18in) MK 108 cannon

Messerschmitt Me 163B-1 Komet

Erprobungskommando 16 operated Me 163B-1 GH+IN (prototype V35) from Bad Zwischenahn, Germany, in 1944. EKdo 16 was the Me 163 test unit, formed at Bad Zwischenahn in summer 1942 and receiving its first Me 163B in May 1944.

operational unit, stationed at Brandis, near Leipzig – attacked a formation of no fewer than 596 B-17 Flying Fortress bombers heading towards the Leuna-Merseburg oil complex.

However, the impact of the rocket fighters was minimal, since the closing speed of around 1300km/h (808mph) meant that the pilot could only employ his two slow-firing MK 108 30mm (1.18in) cannon for three seconds before breaking off the attack (early Me 163B-0 aircraft had been fitted with an alternative armament of two high-velocity 20mm (0.8in) MG 151/20 cannon).

First combat

A first major engagement took place on 16 August, when five Me 163s went up against 1096 US Army Air Force bombers. While the first *Komet* was hit by a B-17's tail-gunner, another *Komet* scored hits on a B-17 of the 305th Bombardment Group, before being destroyed in turn by a P-51 escort fighter. Two days later, pilot Siegfried

Schubert destroyed a pair of B-17s, and other *Komets* took down another two examples of the bomber.

Other weapons options under study included the SG 500 system of upward-firing 50mm (1.96in) shells and wooden underwing racks for up to 24 spin-stabilised R4M rockets.

The problem of providing the *Komet* with adequate firepower was never properly addressed, and production of the Me 163 came to an end in February 1945 after around 400 examples of all variants had been built. Of these, production Me 163B-1a interceptors also joined the other two Gruppen of JG 400, but this would remain the only operational unit to receive the type; its process of re-equipment had been completed by the end of 1944. Eventually, the unit ended the war with only nine confirmed victories.

Variants

Variants of the Me 163 to see limited production included the Me 163S tandem two-seat glider trainer, in which the armament and fuel tanks were removed to provide accommodation for a second seat.

Three examples were completed as the Me 163C-1a, but it seems only one of these ever flew. This variant was an improved Me 163B, with a revised airframe and a modified powerplant to increase powered endurance. There were plans to further refine the basic design to produce the Me 163D that would have featured a retractable tricycle undercarriage, as well as a bubble canopy, larger flaps and automatic wing slats.

A single prototype was completed, and this version was briefly designated Ju 248, reflecting the proposal for quantity manufacture by the Junkers company. When these plans were shelved, the aircraft was re-designated as the Me 263. The prototype was tested by the Soviet Union after the war and its wings and tail surfaces were modified to produce the improved I-270, which flew in 1946 before development was abandoned.

Finally, there were also plans for wartime licence-production of the *Komet* in Japan, where it was to have been produced by Mitsubishi as the Ki-200.

An Me 163B-1a launching at Bad Zwischenahn, home of the trials unit Erprobungskommando 16, which began operating Me 163s in May 1944.

Messerschmitt Me 163B-1 Komet

This Me 163 carries the Baron von Munchausen badge of I Gruppe, Jagdgeschwader 400, based at Brandis near Leipzig, in the Autumn of 1944.

Cockpit
The pilot sat in a primitive cockpit with a reflector gunsight for aiming the cannon. Rear visibility was limited, but this was of little importance when the rocket motor was running.

Armament
The *Komet* was armed with a pair of MK 108 30mm (1.18in) cannon in the wingroots, which gave it a mighty punch. But the high closing speed of the aircraft gave the pilot approximately three seconds firing time.

Landing Gear
As the main wheels were detached from the aircraft shortly after take-off, the Me 163 relied on an extending skid for landing.

Messerschmitt Me 163B-1 Komet

Weight (Maximum take-off) 4310kg (9500lb)

Dimensions Length: 5.85m (19ft 2in), Wingspan: 9.4m (30ft 7in), Height: 2.76m (9ft)

Powerplant One Walter HWK 109-509A rocket motor delivering 14.71 kN (3307lb) of thrust

Speed 955km/h (593mph)

Range 35.5km (22 miles)

Ceiling 12,000m (39,370ft)

Crew 1

Armament Two 30mm (1.18in) MK 108 cannon

Engine
The aircraft was powered by a
single Walter HWK 509A-2 rocket
motor, which would run for about
six minutes on full throttle.

Camouflage
This Me 163B wears the original
camouflage scheme of a green upper
surface, but the fin and rudder have
been newly painted.

Messerschmitt Me 262

The Me 262's place in history is assured by the fact it was the first jet fighter to see combat service anywhere in the world.

Design work on the Me 262 began in late 1938 according to a specification calling for an aircraft powered by a pair of the new gas turbines under development at BMW. After the design was approved, Messerschmitt received a contract for three prototypes each to be powered by two 5.88kN (1323lb) thrust BMW P-3302 turbojets.

The resulting prototypes were characterized by a low-wing monoplane configuration, with the engines mounted below the wing at approximately one-third span. The early prototype Me 262s featured a retractable tailwheel landing gear, superseded by retractable tricycle undercarriage in later prototypes and production aircraft.

Prototype

With BMW experiencing problems with its new jet engine, the initial prototype,

the Me 262 V1, took to the air on 18 April 1941 powered by a single Junkers Jumo 210G piston engine installed in the nose. This proved that the Me 262 had good handling characteristics and on 25 March 1942 the aircraft finally took to the air with BMW 003 turbojets installed – the Jumo 210G was retained in the nose as a backup. Soon after becoming airborne, both of the jet engines failed, and test pilot Fritz Wendel barely managed to complete a circuit and land the Me 262 V1 on the power of the piston engine. The cause of

The Me 262B-1a/U1 night-fighter was created on the basis of the Me 262B-1a dual-control trainer, which differed from the basic fighter in having a second seat in the aft section of an elongated cockpit. Since this resulted in a reduction in internal fuel capacity, auxiliary fuel tanks were added below the forward fuselage.

Messerschmitt Me 262A-1a

A three-view of 'Yellow 8', a Me 262A-1a of 3./JG 7
that was discovered by advancing Allied forces at
Stendal in April 1945. The unit emblem of JG 7 was
a leaping greyhound.

Messerschmitt Me 262A-1a

Weight (Maximum take-off) 6775kg (14,936lb)
Dimensions Length: 10.61m (34ft 9.5in),
Wingspan: 12.50m (41ft 0.12in), Height: 3.8m
(12ft 6.7in)
Powerplant Two 8.8kN (1890lb) Junkers Jumo
004B-1 turbojets
Speed 870km/h (541mph)
Range 845km (525 miles)
Ceiling 11,000m (36,090ft)
Crew 1
Armament Four 30mm (1.18in) cannon

the problem was compressor blade failure, leading to a redesign of the engine and considerable delay to the Me 262 programme. The Me 262 V2, meanwhile, was a test airframe for the fitment of two BMW 003 engines.

Further testing continued with a pair of Junkers turbojets, which were larger and heavier than the BMW units, demanding modification of the airframe. The third prototype, the Me 262 V3, took to the air powered by two 8.24kN (1852lb) thrust Jumo 004A turbojets on 18 July 1942; it was the first of the fighters to be flown by service test pilots. The fourth prototype, Me 262 V4, was similar to V3, while the Me 262 V5 was equipped with two Jumo 004s and a fixed nosewheel.

First series

In early November 1943 the definitive Me 262 V6 prototype was ready to fly on the power of two 8.82kN (1984lb) Jumo 004B-1 turbojets, each of which weighed 91kg (200lb) less than the Jumo 004A. This aircraft also featured the retractable tricycle

Messerschmitt Me 262A-2a

This aircraft flew with 1./Kampfgeschwader 51 'Edelweiss' (KG 51) in March 1945.

landing gear. Ultimately, prototypes and test aircraft were completed up to and including the Me 262 V12. All but the initial Me 262 V1 were powered by Jumo 004A engines.

These were followed by a batch of pre-production Me 262A-0 aircraft that were similarly powered by the Jumo 004A. Of note was the Me 262 V7 that was similar to the V6 but with a redesigned cockpit canopy and cockpit pressurization. Another 23 aircraft were completed as the Me 262A-0 pre-production series, based on the Me 262 V7 standard; most of these were used at the Rechlin test centre and for service trials beginning in late April 1944.

The first series-production Me 262A-1a fighters began to be delivered to the Luftwaffe in July 1944. The designation Me 262A-1b applied to aircraft equipped to carry R4M rockets. A first Me 262 kill was achieved on 15 August 1944 by Helmut Lennartz, the victim a B-17 bomber; Lennartz ultimately ended the war with eight aerial victories flying the jet fighter.

By the end of the conflict, around 1430 examples of the Me 262 had been completed but its arrival was too late to have any impact on the course of the war. Nevertheless, those aircraft

---

Messerschmitt Me 262A-2a

Weight (Maximum take-off) 6387kg (14,080lb)

Dimensions Length: 10.58m (34ft 9in), Wingspan: 12.50m (41ft 0.125in), Height: 3.83m (12ft 6.75in)

Powerplant Two 8.8kN (1890lb) Junkers Jumo 004B-1 turbojets

Speed 870km/h (541mph)

Range 1050km (652 miles)

Ceiling 12,190m (40,000ft)

Crew 1

Armament Two 30mm (1.18in) cannon; plus two 250kg (551lb) bombs under fuselage

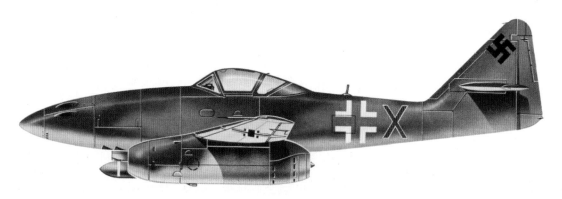

Messerschmitt Me 262B-1a/U1a

Flying with 10 Staffel, Nachtjagdgeschwader 11 (Kommando Walter), the Me 262B-1a/U1 was an interim conversion of a trainer into a nightfighter. Less than a dozen were produced.

that did see combat had an immediate effect, proving to be potent bomber-destroyers, especially when armed with a combination of 24 R4M rockets as well as the four internal 30mm (1.18in) MK 108 cannon.

On the other hand, the Me 262 proved particularly vulnerable to interception by Allied fighters when returning to base, when the type's limited manoeuvrability became a major disadvantage.

Variants

Other variants to see production included the Me 262A-2a fighter-bomber, similar to the Me 262A-1a, but with two racks for 250kg (551lb) bombs and two-gun armament, and the Me 262A-3a intended for close support, with additional armour; this was used mainly for trials work.

The Me 262A-5a was a reconnaissance-fighter version, while the Me 262B-1a was a two-seat conversion trainer with dual flight controls under a redesigned cockpit canopy.

Further developments of the B-series comprised the Me 262B-1a/U1 night fighter with Neptun V (FuG 218) airborne interception radar and the Me 262B-2a two-seat night fighter with additional fuel in a lengthened fuselage.

The Me 262C featured additional rocket boost and was used exclusively for experimental purposes.

Small numbers of Me 262A-1a/U3 recce aircraft entered service. Modified fighters with their cannon removed, these could carry two Rb 50/30 or Rb 20/30 cameras.

Messerschmitt Me 262B-1a/U1

Weight (Maximum take-off) 6387kg (14,080lb)
Dimensions Length: 10.58m (34ft 9in), Wingspan: 12.50m (41ft 0.125in), Height: 3.83m (12ft 6.75in)
Powerplant Two 8.8kN (1890lb) Junkers Jumo 004B-1 turbojets
Speed 870km/h (541mph)
Range 1050km (652 miles)
Ceiling 12,190m (40,000ft)
Crew 1
Armament Four 30mm (1.18in) MK 108 cannon

Messerschmitt Me 262A-1a

Me 262A-1a 'Yellow 7' was on strength with the 11. Staffel of Jagdgeschwader 7, based at Prague in April 1945. The aircraft was eventually captured by the Allies at Lechfeld and is now preserved in the National Air and Space Museum in Washington.

Tail
Control surfaces included fabric-covered elevators, replaced with stronger metal skins on later production aircraft. The powerful rudder was required to maintain directional stability.

Messerschmitt Me 262A-1a
Weight (Maximum take-off) 6775kg (14,936lb)
Dimensions Length: 10.61m (34ft 9.5in), Wingspan: 12.50m (41ft 0.125in), Height: 3.83m (12ft 6.75in)
Powerplant Two 8.8kN (1890lb) Junkers Jumo 004B-1 turbojets
Speed 870km/h (541mph)
Range 845km (525 miles)
Ceiling 11,000m (36,090ft)
Crew 1
Armament Four 30mm (1.18in) MK 108A-3 cannon

Engines
Power was provided by a pair of Junkers Jumo 004B-1 axial-flow turbojets, which suffered from poor reliability and limited service life, primarily due to the effect of Allied bombing on production facilities, and the lack of certain materials required for the turbine blades.

Pilot
'Yellow 7' was flown by Heinz Arnold, who
had scored 42 victories flying piston-engined
fighters before transitioning to the jet. He
scored seven jet kills in just three weeks before
being posted missing in April 1945.

Guns
Standard fixed armament comprised four 30mm
(1.18in) Rheinmetall Borsig MK 108A-3 cannon,
with 100 rounds for each of the upper guns and
80 rounds for the lower guns.

Heinkel He 162 *Volksjäger*

The Heinkel He 162 was developed and flown in an extraordinarily short period of time, the factory requiring only 38 days between receiving detailed drawings and the maiden flight of a prototype on 6 December 1944.

On its first flight, this turbojet-engined interceptor demonstrated a top speed of 840km/h (520mph). The aircraft had been devised by Nazi officials as a *Volksjäger* ('people's fighter'). From the outset it was intended to be small, agile enough to outmanoeuvre numerically superior Allied fighter opposition, and requiring only limited skilled labour and minimal scarce strategic materials for its manufacture.

A requirement for the new jet fighter was issued on 8 September 1944, and Heinkel received the official go-ahead to proceed with its P.1073 design on the 30th of that month, gaining the contract over their rival Blohm und Voss's P.211.

The company planned an initial output of a 1000 aircraft per month.

Controversial choice

Despite high-ranking Nazi officials supporting the emergency fighter programme, it faced criticism from leading Luftwaffe figures, including fighter ace Adolf Galland, who was among those arguing for continued support for the Me 262 rather than

Heinkel He 162 V-1

The first prototype, He 162 V1, crashed at Schwechat Airfield, Vienna, on 10 December 1944, in front of an invited audience of high-ranking Nazi officials. The pilot, *Flugkapitän* Gotthold Peter, was killed.

fuselage of light alloy, with a semi-circular monocoque structure and a moulded plywood nose. The cockpit featured an upward-hinged canopy and cartridge-actuated ejection seat. The wheels and brakes were taken from the Messerschmitt Bf 109G, and the powerplant was a single BMW 003 turbojet, mounted directly above the high-mounted wing.

Prototype development

Although the initial prototype of the initial He 162A was lost in an accident on 10 December 1944, development continued and revealed a number of aerodynamic shortcomings. In particular, the levels of lateral and directional instability were unacceptable, with tight left-hand turns being a notable problem. Furthermore, the use of acids in

Heinkel He 162 V-1

Weight (Maximum take-off) 2000kg (4410lb)

Dimensions Length: 9.05m (29ft 8in), Wingspan: 7.2m (23ft 7in), Height: 2.6m (8ft 6in)

Powerplant One BMW-109-003E-1 Sturm axial flow jet engine, 800kg (1,764lb) static thrust

Speed 840km/h (520mph) at sea level

Range 975km (606 miles)

Ceiling 12,000m (39,000ft)

Crew 1

Armament Two 20mm (0.8in) MG 151/20 cannon

the aircraft's construction led to the appearance of some structural damage on the early prototypes.

The aerodynamic issues were addressed in the third and fourth prototypes, both of which were flown on 16 January 1945. These featured a slightly enlarged tail and wingtips tilted downwards at an anhedral angle of 55 degrees. Also in January, a first batch of aircraft was delivered to a Luftwaffe unit for operational evaluation and service trials took place – the unit in question was Jagdgeschwader 3's Erprobungskommando 162, based at Rechlin and commanded by Heinz Bär (who would end the war with 220 victories).

He 162A-0

In the meantime, a total of 10 prototype He 162As were completed (He 162 V1 to V10), and these were also considered pre-production He 162A-0 aircraft. Production was centred upon the Heinkel factory at Vienna-Schwechat, with plans to expand to multiple manufacturing locations – including the use of slave labour and underground facilities – for the series-built He 162A-1.

Once the manufacturing effort was in full swing – with facilities also at Rostock-Marienehe, Bernburg and at Mittelwerke in the Harz mountains

– it was anticipated that monthly output would reach as many as 6000 airframes. A first frontline unit, Jagdgeschwader 1, was equipped with 50 initial-production He 162A-1 aircraft at Leck in northern Germany on 4 May 1945, this formation consisting of a single Gruppe comprising three squadrons. However, British forces occupied the airfield on 8 May and the unit was forced to surrender; by this time, a second Gruppe, II./JG 1, had also began its conversion to the type, its pilots undergoing training on the *Salamander* at Rechlin.

It had been planned for the *Volksjäger* units to be manned by Hitler Youth pilots who had undergone only minimum training in gliders before progressing to the frontline jet units. In the event, these plans were thwarted by the chaos and confusion of the final months of the Third Reich, as well as a lack of fuel.

He 162A-2

The bulk of production encompassed the He 162A-2, which differed in terms of armament. While the original requirement was for one or two 30mm

Heinkel He 162 V-10

The tenth prototype Salamander was flown by the Erprobungskommando 162, the test unit for the type, based at Rechlin in Germany.

Heinkel He 162 V-10

Weight (Maximum take-off) 2800kg (6173lb)

Dimensions Length: 9.05m (29ft 8in), Wingspan: 7.2m (23ft 7in), Height: 2.6m (8ft 6in)

Powerplant One BMW-109-003E-1 Sturm axial flow jet engine, 800kg (1,764lb) static thrust

Speed 840km/h (520mph) at sea level

Range 975km (606 miles)

Ceiling 12,000m (39,000ft)

Crew 1

Armament Two 30mm (1.18in) MK 108 cannon

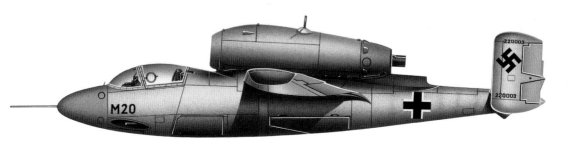

Heinkel He 162A-1

'White 4' was operated by a frontline unit, 1./Jagdgeschwader 1, based at Leck. This particular aircraft, *Werknummer* 120097, was captured by the Allies and tested by the RAF after the war.

(1.18in) cannon, the He 162 V1 first prototype had been built around a pair of 20mm (0.8in) MG 151/20 weapons, offering greater ammunition capacity. While the He 162 V6 prototype had been armed with a pair of 30mm (1.18in) MK 108s, intended for the He 162A-1, in the He 162A-2 the armament was switched back to two MG 151/20s, with a consequent reduction in airframe vibration; each gun was provided with 120 rounds.

A total of 116 He 162s were built and more than 800 were in various stages of assembly when their production facilities were captured by the Allies. While the He 162 is today remembered as the *Salamander*, it should be noted that this was the codename for the overall manufacturing programme in Germany and was popularised after the war by the Allies. In contrast, Heinkel referred to the jet fighter as the *Spatz* ('Sparrow').

Heinkel He 162A-1
Weight (Maximum take-off) 2800kg (6173lb)
Dimensions Length: 9.05m (29ft 8in), Wingspan: 7.2m (23ft 7in), Height: 2.6m (8ft 6in)
Powerplant One BMW-109-003E-1 Sturm axial flow jet engine, 800kg (1,764lb) static thrust
Speed 889km/h (553mph) at sea level (with emergency boosted thrust)
Range 975km (606 miles)
Ceiling 12,000m (39,000ft)
Crew 1
Armament Two 30mm (1.181in) MK 108 cannon

This underground facility was located in Hinterbrühl, Austria, and produced 40–50 He 162s per month. Total production reached about 320 units before the end of the war. This photograph was taken by American forces after the factory was captured in April 1945.

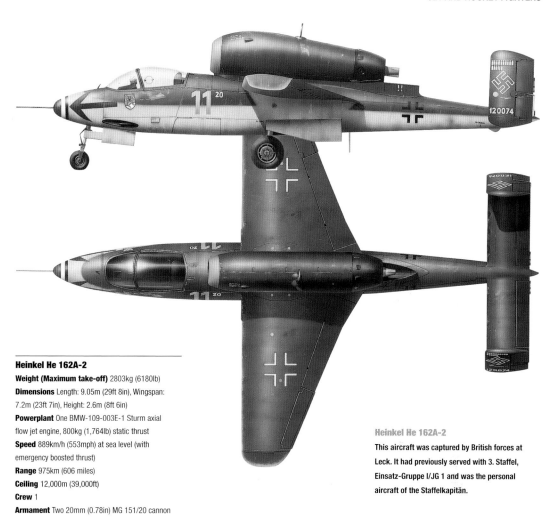

Heinkel He 162A-2

Weight (Maximum take-off) 2803kg (6180lb)

Dimensions Length: 9.05m (29ft 8in), Wingspan: 7.2m (23ft 7in), Height: 2.6m (8ft 6in)

Powerplant One BMW-109-003E-1 Sturm axial flow jet engine, 800kg (1,764lb) static thrust

Speed 889km/h (553mph) at sea level (with emergency boosted thrust)

Range 975km (606 miles)

Ceiling 12,000m (39,000ft)

Crew 1

Armament Two 20mm (0.78in) MG 151/20 cannon

Heinkel He 162A-2

This aircraft was captured by British forces at Leck. It had previously served with 3. Staffel, Einsatz-Gruppe I/JG 1 and was the personal aircraft of the Staffelkapitän.

Bachem Ba 349 *Natter*

The remarkable Ba 349 emerged from an urgent requirement for a point-defence interceptor to protect Germany from the massed Allied bombing raids that were commonplace by early 1944.

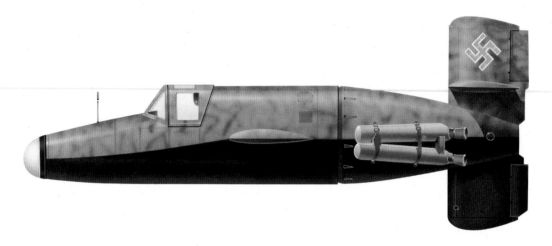

Heinkel, Junkers, Messerschmitt and Bachem were all recipients of a specification for a cheap and semi-expendable piloted missile, but it was the latter firm's BP 20 *Natter* ('Adder') that was chosen for development, with the official designation Ba 349.

The design team led by Erich Bachem devised a fairly crude airframe that could be built by unskilled woodworkers, with no need for complex jigs or tooling. The short wings lacked ailerons, lateral control instead being provided by differential use of the elevators.

The fuselage accommodated the one-man cockpit and a Walter 109-509A-2 sustainer rocket developing 16.67kN (3748lb) of thrust for 70 seconds at full power. Intended to be launched vertically, the Natter would be propelled initially by four Schmidding 109-553 solid-fuel boosters, each producing 11.77kN

Bachem Ba 349

The Ba 349 was one of a number of ingenious projects intended to stem the Allied bombing campaign. It was intended to be vertically launched, the pilot and aircraft being recovered afterwards by parachute.

(2646lb) of thrust for 10 seconds, before they were jettisoned.

Trials

The first of 15 Ba 349 test airframes was ready to begin trials work in October 1944. Initial evaluation took the form of towed, unpowered flights behind a Heinkel He 111. After further glider tests, an unmanned flight using the booster rockets only was achieved in December 1944. By January, the programme had progressed to unmanned launches using both the boosters and the sustainer rocket. However, the first piloted vertical launch ended in disaster, when test pilot Lothar

Bachem Ba 349

Weight (Maximum take-off) 2232kg (4921lb)

Dimensions Length: 6m (19ft 8in), Wingspan: 4m (13ft 1in), Height: 2.25m (7ft 5in)

Powerplant One Walter HWK 109-509A-2 sustainer rocket, 16.67kN (3748lbf) thrust (70 second full power); four Schmidding 109-553 solid-fuel boosters, 11.77kN (2646lbf) thrust (10 seconds)

Speed 1000km/h (620mph)

Range 55km (34 miles) after climbing at 6000m (19,685ft)

Ceiling 12,000m (39,000ft)

Crew 1

Armament 24 × 73mm (2.874in) Henschel Hs 297 Föhn rocket shells

Siebert was killed on 23 February 1945. The accident occurred as a result of the cockpit canopy becoming detached in flight, after which the aircraft dived into the ground from a height of around 1525m (5000ft).

Attack mode

It seems this was the only attempt at a manned, powered flight of the *Natter*. Had the programme developed further, operational tactics called for a vertical launch on autopilot, the pilot taking control of the aircraft when positioned above the enemy bomber stream. After assuming a shallow dive onto the target, the Ba 349 would have been armed by jettisoning the nose cone to expose a battery of 24 73mm (2.87in) Henschel Hs 217 Föhn or 33 55mm (2.17in) R4M unguided rockets.

After these had been fired, the aircraft would break away from the battle and the pilot would prepare to bale out. This was achieved by jettisoning the nose section, separating it from the rest of the fuselage. The pilot would be extracted by the deceleration of the rear section as it deployed a braking parachute, leaving him to descend under his own parachute. The rear fuselage would also be recovered to reuse the Walter rocket motor.

Production

A total of 200 examples of the Ba 349A initial-production version were ordered, with plans for these to be split between Luftwaffe and SS units, and around 20 examples were completed but not used operationally.

The Ba 349B was to have been an improved version with a larger wing, more powerful sustainer rocket, additional fuel capacity and a pair of 30mm (1.18in) cannon added to the armament.

A Natter is prepared for launch. Following a cockpit canopy malfunction, test pilot Lothar Siebert was killed during the first piloted launch on 28 February 1945.

Glossary

Aufklärung	Reconnaissance	Generalfeldmarschall	General of the Air Force/Marshal of the RAF
Ausbildungs-	Training	Generalleutnant	Major-General/Air Vice Marshal
		Generalmajor	Brigadier-General/Air Commodore
Befehlshaber	Commander	Generaloberst	General/Air Chief Marshal
Behelfs	Auxiliary	Geschwader	Equivalent to Allied Group
Beobachter	Observer/Navigator	Geschwaderkommodore	Geschwader commander
Bodenlafette	Ventral gun mount	Gruppe	Equivalent to Allied Wing
Bordkanone	Fixed aircraft cannon	Gruppenkommandeur	Group commander
Bordfliegerstaffel	Shipborne aircraft squadron		
Bramo	Brandenburgische Motoren Werke	Hauptmann	Captain/Flight Lieutenant
B-Schule	Advanced/Blind Flying Training School	Heeres-	Army
B-Stand	Dorsal gunner's position	Heeresaufklärungstaffel	Army or Tactical Reconnaissance Squadron
Buna	Synthetic rubber (originally a trade name)	Himmelbet	'Heavenly Bed' – Night ground-controlled intercept zone
C-Schule	Advanced Flying Training School, multi-engine	HWK	Helmuth Walter Werke
C-Stand	Ventral gunner's position		
		Jabo	Jagdbomber
DFS	Deutsches Forschungsinstitut für Segelflug	Jabo-Rei	Jagdbomber mit vergrosster reichweite
		Jagd-	Fighter (Hunt, Chase, Pursuit)
Einsatzkommando	Combat Operations Detachment	Jagdbomber	Fighter bomber
EJG	Ergänzungs-Jagdgeschwader	Jagdfliegerführer	Fighter Command
EKdo	Erprobungs Kommando	Jagdfliegerschule	Fighter Training School
Elektrische Trägervorrichtung	Electrically-operated bomb racks	Jafü	Jagdfliegerführer
Entwicklungs-	Development-	Jagdgeschwader	Fighter Group
Ergänzungs-	Replacement-	Jagdgruppe	Fighter Wing
Ergänzungs-Jagdgeschwader	Fighter Replacement Training Group	Jagdstaffel	Fighter Squadron
Ersatz	Substitute or Replacement	JG	Jagdgeschwader
		JGr	Jagdgruppe
FA	Ferngesteuerte Anlage	JFS	Jagdfliegerschule
FAGr	Fernaufklärungsgruppe	Jumo	Junkers Motoren Werke
Fallschirmjäger	Paratroopers		
Fernaufklärung	Long-range Reconnaissance	Kampf	Battle (Bomber, when applied to aircraft)
Fernaufklärungsgruppe	Long-range Reconnaissance Gruppe	Kampfbeobachter	Artillery Observer
Fernaufklärungstaffel	Long-range reconnaissance Squadron	Kampfgeschwader	Bomber Group
Fernnachtjagd	Long-range night fighter/intruder	Kampfgeschwader zur	Special Duty/Transport Group
Fernzielgerät	Remote aiming device or bombsight	Kampfgruppe	Bomber Wing
FFS	Flugzeugführerschule	Kdo	Kommando
FHL	Ferngerichtete Hecklafette	Kette	Flight of three aircraft
Flak	Fliegerabwehrkanone	KG	Kampfgeschwader
Flieger	Pilot (as description) or Airman (as rank)	KGr	Kampfgruppe
Fliegerabwehrkanone	Anti-Aircraft Gun/Artillery	KGzbV	Kampfgeschwader zur besonderen Verwendung
Fliegerdivision	Air Division	Koluft	Kommander der Luftwaffe bei einen AOK
Fliegerkorps	Air Corps	Kommando	Detachment
Flugberietschaft	Duty Flight attached to higher formations	Kü.Fl	Küsten Flieger
Flugzeugführerschule	Pilot/Aircraft Commander School	Küsten Flieger	Coastal Aviation
FuG	Funkgerät		
Funkgerät	Radio or Radar set	Langstrecken-	Long-range
Führerkurierstaffel	Führer's courier squadron	Lastensiegler	Cargo glider
Führungsstab	Operations Staff	Lehr-	Instruction
		Lehrgeschwader	Demonstration/Operational development Group
General	Lieutenant General or Air Marshal	Luftflotte	Air Fleet
General der Jagdflieger	General of Fighters	Lufttorpedo	Air-dropped Torpedo
General der Kampfflieger	General of Bombers	Lufttransportstaffel	Air Transport Squadron

Luftwaffe	Air Force
Luftwaffenführungsstab	Luftwaffe Operations Staff
Luftwaffengeneralstab	Luftwaffe Air Staff
Major	Major/Squadron Leader
Maschinengewehr	Machine Gun
Maschinenkanone	Machine Cannon
MG	*Maschinengewehr*
Minensuchgruppe	Minehunting/sweeping wing
Mistel	(Mistletoe) – combination aircraft
MK	*Maschinenkanone*
MW 50	Methanol-water mix
Nachtjagd-	Night Fighter
Nachtjagdgeschwader	Night Fighter Group
Nachtschlacht-	Night Harassment
Nachtschlachtgruppe	Night Harassment Wing
NAGr	*Nahaufklärungsgruppe*
Nahaufklärungs-	Short-range reconnaissance
Nahaufklärungsgruppe	Short-range reconnaissance group
NJG	*Nachtjagdgeschwader*
NSGr	*Nachtschlachtgruppe*
Ob.d.L	*Oberbefehlshaber der Luftwaffe*
Ob.d.M	*Oberbefehlshaber der Marine*
Oberbefehlshaber der	
Luftwaffe	Commander-in-Chief of the Luftwaffe
Oberbefehlshaber der Marine	Commander-in-Chief of the Navy
Oberfeldwebel	Master Sergeant/Flight Sergeant
Oberkommando des Heeres	Army High Command
Oberkommando der Luftwaffe	Air Force High Command
Oberkommando der Marine	Navy High Command
Oberkommando der	
Wehrmacht	High Command of the Armed Forces
Oberleutnant	First Lieutenant/Flying Officer
Oberst	Colonel/Group Captain
Oberstleutnant	Lieutenant Colonel/Wing Commander
OKH	*Oberkommando des Heeres*
OKL	*Oberkommando der Luftwaffe*
OKM	*Oberkommando der Marine*
OKW	*Oberkommando der Wehrmacht*
Rauchgerät	Rocket-booster unit
R-Gerät	*Rauchgerät*
Rotte	A flight of two aircraft
R-Stoff	Rocket fuel (57% Monoxylidene, 43% triethylamine)
Rüstatz	Field conversion kit
SAGr	*See-Aufklärungsgruppe*
Sanitätsstaffel	Air Ambulance Squadron
Sch.G	*Schlachtgeschwader*
Schlacht-	Close-support/Assault
Schlachtgeschwader	Close Support Group
Schlepp-	Towing
Schnellkampfgeschwader	High-speed Bomber/Attack Group

Schwarm	Flight of four fighters
Schnellbomber	Fast bomber
Schräge Musik	'Slanting' or 'Jazz Music' – cannon firing obliquely upwards
SD	Splitterbomb, Dickwand
Sd.Kdo	Special Detachment
Seeaufklärungsgruppe	Maritime Reconnaissance Wing
Seenotsdienst	Air Sea Rescue Service
Seenotsstaffel	Air Sea Rescue Squadron
SG	*Schlachtgeschwader*
SKG	*Schnellkampfgeschwader*
Sonder-	Special purpose
Spanner-Anlage	Early infra-red sensor system
S-Stoff	Rocket fuel (97% Nitric Acid, 3% Sulphuric Acid)
Stab-	Staff
Stabschwarm	Staff flight in a *Gruppe*
Staffel	Squadron
Staffelkapitan	Squadron commander
St.G	*Sturzkampfgeschwader*
Störkampfstaffel	Night Harassment Squadron
Stuka	*Sturzkampfflugzeug*
Sturm-	Assault
Sturmgruppe	Assault Wing
Sturzkampfflugzeug	Dive bomber
Sturzkampfgeschwader	Dive bomber Group
Sturz-visier	Dive Bombing Sight
Trägergeschwader	Aircraft Carrier Group
Troika-schlepp	Triple tow (of large gliders by three aircraft)
Umbau	Reconstruction
Umrüst-Bausatz	Factory conversion kit
V	*Versuchs* (Experimental)
Verband	Formation
Verstellschraube	Variable pitch propeller
VS	*Verstellschraube*
Werfer-Granate	Grenade projector/rocket propelled shell
Wettererkundungsstaffel	Meteorological squadron
Wfr.Gr	*Werfer-Granate*
X-Gerät	Electronic blind-flying/bombing aid
Y-Gerät	Electronic blind-flying/range-finding aid
Zwilling	Twin or coupled
Zerstörer	Destroyer, or heavy fighter
Zerstörergeschwader	Heavy Fighter Group
ZG	*Zerstörergeschwader*

Luftwaffe fighter losses: 1943–44

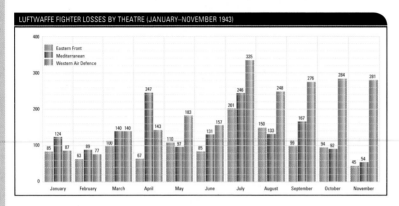

LUFTWAFFE FIGHTER LOSSES BY THEATRE (JANUARY–NOVEMBER 1943)

At the end of 1943, German fighter production was at just over 700 planes per month and rising. By the end of 1943, the Luftwaffe was losing over 280 aircraft a month in the defence of the Reich – though this was down from a July high of 335. These losses, combined with the other theatres, represented over 20 per cent of operational losses per month – down from 42 per cent in October (second Schweinfurt raid) but still high. And it was only getting worse for the Germans; their industry was being pounded but they had no way of attacking their enemies. By the end of 1943, the Germans could not mount a bomber raid against the British, to say nothing of the Soviets or Americans.

1944: The Decisive Year

At the beginning of the year, the Luftwaffe had just under 1100 fighters available for combat, with about half in the West and the other half scattered throughout other theatres: the Eastern Front, the Mediterranean and Norway.

These fighters faced less than 900 operational American bombers (1200 aircraft but only 882 ready crews) and another 1200 British bombers of all types (including 650 Lancasters and 300 Halifaxes). However, the war of attrition was in favour of the Allies. Whereas the Germans were producing about 500 single-engine fighters per month, the Americans alone were adding 1000 bombers to their inventory. And German

production was being bombed, while American production was unimpeded by the war.

Also, by the start of the year, the Americans had finally unlocked the secrets of long-range fighter escort with a relatively simple solution: drop tanks. The fighters (primarily P-51s) carried external fuel into combat, and jettisoned the external tanks when they entered combat. The result was that the escorts provided protection to the bombers throughout entire missions. The addition of 1100 American fighters to the above bomber totals equalled a 4:1 ratio in favour of the US bomber offensive into Germany.

American bomber raids shifted targets early in the new year. With the planned invasion of the Continent, the Americans decided that German aircraft production was the most important target, in order to destroy the Luftwaffe and gain air superiority. By February 1944, a massive effort was aimed at the destruction of German aircraft production.

'Big Week'

'Big Week' (20–25 February 1944) brought massive attacks against German fighters, with the Eighth Air Force (from Britain) and the Fifteenth Air Force (from Italy) flying more than 3000 and 500 sorties respectively and dropping 10,160 tonnes (10,000 tons) of bombs. The mission was ultimately successful; for the loss of around 200 American

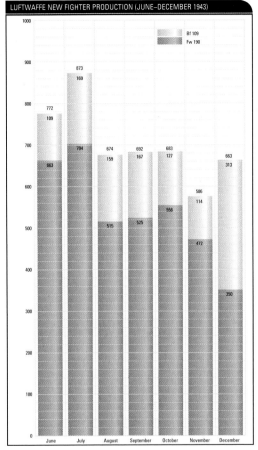

LUFTWAFFE NEW FIGHTER PRODUCTION (JUNE–DECEMBER 1943)

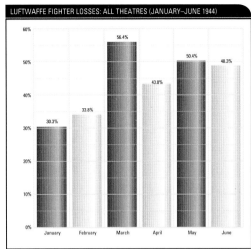

LUFTWAFFE FIGHTER LOSSES: ALL THEATRES (JANUARY–JUNE 1944)

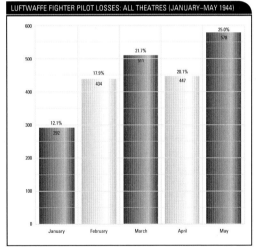

LUFTWAFFE FIGHTER PILOT LOSSES: ALL THEATRES (JANUARY–MAY 1944)

aircraft, most of the Luftwaffe twin-engine fighter groups were destroyed, and the Germans lost an additional 100 single-engine pilots and planes, plus a further 200 on the ground (at airfields or in production). To use another metric, American losses of under seven per cent destroyed almost 20 per cent of the Luftwaffe's day-fighter force. And the Allies continued to dominate in the air. Allied numbers climbed while German numbers declined.

By June, the Allies were pressing the Luftwaffe hard. At the start of the month, the Allies in the West had increased their numbers to over 2750 bombers and 1250 fighters available for combat, plus another 1250 British bombers. Once again these numbers were increasing, but the important factor is that losses were declining. The Germans were simply shooting down fewer aircraft. The defenders, understandably, had fewer aircraft, with only 991 fighters available on 1 June 1944 to combat the Allied forces. These comprised 788 single-engine and 203 twin-engine machines, but with only 472 and 83 pilots, respectively, fit for operations.

Index

Picture Credits

PHOTOGRAPHS:

AirSeaLandPhotos: 8, 11,16, 22, 58, 71, 87, 92, 100, 116, 119

Amber Books/Aerospace: 6, 7, 20, 25–53 all, 60–68 all, 78–85 all, 88, 94–99 all, 105–111 all

ARTWORKS:

Amber Books/Aerospace: 10, 11, 13–49 all, 52–56 all, 62 top, 64/65, 68–69 all, 84, 85, 91, 102–118 all

David Bocquelet: 61, 62 bottom, 63, 66, 67, 70, 72–74 all, 77–79 all, 93–99 all, 123–124 all

Ed Jackson – artbyedo.com: 5, 12, 50, 51, 57, 71, 86–90 all, 92

Murilo Martins: 75–76 all, 80–83 all